# A Question of Faith

*October, 1909 —*

# A QUESTION OF FAITH

BY

## L. DOUGALL

AUTHOR OF " BEGGARS' ALL," " THE ZEIT GEIST," ETC.

BOSTON AND NEW YORK
HOUGHTON, MIFFLIN AND COMPANY
The Riverside Press, Cambridge
1895

*The Riverside Press, Cambridge, Mass., U. S. A.*
Electrotyped and Printed by H. O. Houghton & Co.

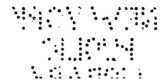

*"According to your faith*
*be it done unto you"*

# A QUESTION OF FAITH

## CHAPTER I

On a mild day in February, an English gentleman, by name Matthew Knighton, was walking across a bit of moorland on the borders of his own estate. He was bound for a neighboring hamlet to meet a friend who was expected to arrive there by the weekly coach, which at this season was the only public means of passenger transport in the locality.

Knighton had just ascended a short steep hill to reach the upland which he was now crossing. Before him, stretching in ridge beyond ridge, green fore-ground merging into gray and misty distance, was one of the great moors that lie south of the Bristol Channel.

His path was a narrow cart-road. On either side the turf, wherever it was seen, was of very vivid and tender green, by reason of moss that grew thickly in the grass; but on the greater part of the ground, heather with its brown seeds, and gorse with a few winter blossoms, were the covering. A few minutes brought him to where, in a hollow of the undulating ground near the descent of a steep combe, half a dozen old cottages were falling into ruins. There was no sign of life about any of these hovels except one, in the door of which stood an old woman who appeared to be the only inhabitant of the place, unless a jackdaw with clipped wings, who hopped at her feet, could be looked upon as her companion.

The old woman's eye was still bright and her features shapely, although her skin was withered, wrinkled, and brown. She was dressed in such garments as an old witch might wear. She no sooner saw who was coming than she waved the stick she held with a sort of majestic welcome.

"Well, what now?" asked Knighton, with testy tolerance, arrested, when he came near, by this peculiar demonstration.

He was a man perhaps about fifty, with iron-gray hair and shaven face; he was not above medium height, but strong both of feature and of limb; he looked like a country gentleman who did not often bestir himself to go up to town, but he looked also as if he brought what was best in town down to him, for in his face there was no lack of that keener intelligence which mental activity gives.

This middle-aged man and aged woman stood facing one another on the windy moor, the one possessing all the advantage of what is called education and good breeding; the other, nothing but what nature had bestowed of long experience and wit. And yet they were not altogether unlike, these two; many encounters had given to each a sort of rough conception that they two looked out upon the world of men around them from very similar standpoints.

"I 'll tell 'ee a thing I 've been a-thinken of, zir. There 's beätles as crawl about; they 've got feälers, zoo they can knaw where they be going an' what they be doing. If half the beätles wer' a-given no feälers, an' had to run among them as has, would that be right and vair?"

"Very hard on them, Gor, I should say."

"But moäst o' men are a-made thèt way zhure enough, an' it 's no vault to them thet they know no moor of God or man than they can zee and 'ear and zmell — beätles wi'out feälers they be. Is it right and vair?"

The Squire meditated a moment. He was accustomed to have many questions brought to him to decide, but perhaps few as congenial.

"Their forefathers neglected to use the feelers that were given them; they grew weak and dropped off, so their children had none."

He looked, not without a good deal of inward curiosity, to see how far the shrewd old woman would understand.

"Oh, thee be allus a-squaring things for th' Almighty for us poor volks; but don't tell I — I zay it 's not vair."

Knighton went on his way over a ridge of hill.

When the coach stopped, it put down only one passenger and his luggage. He was a young man, and, seen at a little distance, he was quite like the ordinary young man that one sees in the illustrations of magazine stories. That is to say, his clothes were made by a good tailor, his features were regular, and his hair and mustache were just what they ought to be. Observed more closely, he had, of course, an individuality; it would have been natural to suppose that he was a person of good taste and good feeling, probably strongly actuated by both. Knighton greeted him.

"Good of you to come," said the traveler. "A tremendous comfort to see some one person I know. Old Crusoe, marching out of the waves, could n't have been much more *in terra incognita* than I am." He spoke in a rather excited way, as if his speech was more wordy than usual.

"Will you walk?" asked the other. "You will want to stretch your legs; and the trap has a circuit to make."

The two men started back upon the path across the moor.

The younger man's name was Henry Harvey. He was an artist. Although descended from a family of this neighborhood, he had never visited the place before. It was he who spoke.

"When my father and I met you in town you were so tremendously kind that I feel as if I must talk to you a bit about this affair. I hope it won't bore you; you see you know her so well; and about the place and everything. You see, theoretically I don't believe in being married by family arrangement, and neither, of course, does my cousin Alice; but we've had to write a good many letters to one another. Hang me if I'm not half bowled over, and I think Alice " —

"Is favorably inclined toward you."

"Well, apart from the question of liking, it is a decidedly good arrangement for us both. The rents here are barely enough for her to scratch along on, and I would like to have the old place and can afford to keep it up."

Here no remark came in answer. Harvey, who was sensitive to approval or disapproval, began again.

"You see, of course, we don't mean to dispense with love, but I was merely showing why, liking each other as we do, Alice might think it worth while to come and have a try for it."

"Quite a situation for a novel."

"Yes, isn't it; only, some way, in real life things never smack of romance as they do in books — at least not until they are long past: there is too much detail, too much or too little personal responsibility, I don't know which. But, you know, of course it all depends on Miss Bolitho. You have known her all her life, and, to tell the

truth, I am frightened at her character. I
know she has been up to Cambridge like
a man, and taken a degree, or whatever
they give the feminines. Is she appallingly
strong-minded?"

"By strong-minded do you mean " —

"Oh — wearing big boots, you know, and
a top-coat, and pot-hat, and " —

"The strength of Miss Bolitho's clothing
is, as far as I have observed, proportioned to
the severity of the weather and her need to
expose herself to it. If by ' the strength of
her mind ' you mean the strength of her will,
I should think that, also, would be brought
into force only when it was required."

"Is she such a paragon? A fellow wrote
to me the other day, and said that his wife
had no faults, but she was also very nice;
and that the ' but ' was not inadvertent.
And there is something in that view of it,
you know; it 's the best proof, I always say,
of the ' Adam's fall ' story that we can't
even conceive of a person being charming
and faultless."

Knighton spoke mildly. "Faultlessness, then, in your idea involves one of those two greatest faults against God and man, — insipidity or arrogance?"

"But about Miss Bolitho — she wrote to me that she was not religious. That is the worst of modern women — not being religious."

"All women in other ages you conceive to have been devout and holy?"

"Well, she meant she was an agnostic or something. Now, I am not grand at religion, but I had about as soon hang myself as believe that things were bounded by the evidence of my senses."

"I do not know that ' agnostic ' applies to her in its exact meaning."

"Hang it, if I have used the word wrongly! I am just like the lady who met the vicar after he had given a lecture on the Gnostics, and said that she was so much obliged to him, for she had never known precisely what agnostics were before."

They passed the cottages where the witch

lived, and just beyond they left the road by
which Knighton had come an hour before,
keeping to a path running beside a combe,
that here cut into the hill over which they
were walking. The sides of the combe
were not bare, but thickly wooded with a
low growth of oak which still retained its
sere leaves; and although among them in
some places hollies grew luxuriant, the
myriad of dead leaves and the grotesque
shapes of the roots of a former generation
of oaks, out of which, in many cases, the
younger trees grew, gave the hollow a pecul-
iarly desolate appearance. A stream which
gathered in the higher hill above was seen
pitching down the rocky centre of the place,
and heard after it ceased to be seen.

At the edge of the wood the path again
divided into two. The one led downward
along the side of the combe, about halfway
between the stream and the summit, but
the trees were so thick that a little way
below neither path nor stream could be descried from the top; the other path led on,

through some cultivated fields, over the open brow of the bluff on which they were. It was this that Knighton took. Harvey, who had been observing the prospect with eager eyes, felt disappointment.

"What a shame our way does not lie down there! What a romantic place!" Then after a pause, in which the rugged grandeur of the moor above, the soft color of the leaves of the wood and strange shapes of its roots, grew upon him, he added, with some quiet strength of purpose in his tone, "I will make a picture of that."

"In summer?" said Knighton.

"No; now. Look at the grays of that sky. Look at the mass of tawny leaves and the stream" —

"And kill yourself — you, unaccustomed to a damp climate."

"It *is* bleak up here in the wind."

"Nothing to-day to what it usually is."

"Nevertheless, I will make the picture."

There was something about him when he spoke of the picture that commanded Knighton's respect. He spoke in a more cordial tone.

"As a matter of fact we can get to Norcombe as well by the lower path, but farther down it runs rather narrow at the edge of a steep bit of rock. It is hardly safe in my opinion. In any case it is a shut-in place. I prefer the open."

This prosaic preference jarred on Harvey's tastes; he did not listen intently to what Knighton went on to say; the idea of the new picture had taken possession of him. The artistic faculty is stimulated just in proportion as the whole mind is stimulated. Harvey had, as it were, lately fallen heir to an engagement of marriage with his second cousin Miss Bolitho — in so far, at least, as a will can entail such an engagement. He had come quickly to ratify or cancel the arrangement. He was deeply excited; at the very source of all his ordinary thoughts and feelings life was pulsing more strongly; and that his art was an integral part of him was proved in this —

that he was now more perfectly an artist than at ordinary seasons. He looked back lingeringly at the place he had chosen, as they walked on.

Behind them, as they now walked, the higher ridge of the moorland rose with its vivid greens of moss and gray greens of wintry heaths; before them, below the descent, could be seen the low meadows of the valley of Norcombe, to which they were bound. Beyond that, again, another hill rose, gray because it was well-wooded and leafless. Before they came to the descent they stopped at a good-sized cottage or small farmhouse, the only house on the hill. It was a lonely place, but its inmates had no appearance of leading a solitary life. They were a stalwart, peaceful, country couple, who in summer let their best rooms to such chance tourists as might wish to explore the beauty of the secluded neighborhood. Knighton had stopped at the cottage on business of his own. While they tarried, Harvey learned these particulars.

"I will take these rooms," he said to Knighton. "I can live here as well as at Norcombe Inn, and I can make my picture."

Knighton raised his eyebrows. "You will be farther from Norcombe," he said.

"Just at present I am a good deal more frightened of Norcombe than of any other place in the wide world. And, look here, you won't desert me this evening; you promised to let me make my first visit under your protection. I am really very much alarmed, you know. Just put yourself in my place! But I suppose you are one of those very magnificent fellows who would never be frightened of a woman."

There was nothing in Knighton's face that expressed either assent or denial with regard to the flattery thus thrust at him.

Harvey engaged his lodging. After that he walked on with Knighton down to the village of Norcombe, to the inn whither his luggage had been sent.

## CHAPTER II

THAT same afternoon, an hour later,
Alice Bolitho came downstairs in the old
house which had lately come into her possession, and showed herself at the door of a
lower sitting-room, equipped for walking.
Inside the sitting-room sat a lady who might
still properly be described as a young lady,
except that the wearing of a wedding-ring
and tokens of widowhood in the black dress
prevented the conventional use of that term.

"Alice!" (in great surprise) "are you
going out? Oh, I don't think I would if I
were you; you know you might meet —
Do you think it would seem quite ladylike,
dear, to go out to meet him? He would be
sure to *think that*, you know."

"If he did, I should think him a duffer,
and which would be the worse? You are
always alarmed, my pretty Amy, about

what other people will think; but you never get up any very great alarms about what you and I may think of them, which is quite as important."

"Oh, if I were you, Alice, I wouldn't begin by thinking that he is this or that. I would just try to make him think me as nice as I could."

"Yes" (good-naturedly), "I am sure that is just what you would do if you were I; and I suppose it is what you will do, not being I."

The other, not being very quick of mind, did not take in the point of the retort; a smiling manner was more to her than the precise meaning of words.

"I don't think you had better go out until he has called; it would *seem*, you know, as if you were in a hurry to see him."

"On the contrary, it is because he will probably call that I am going out to avoid him. That is ladylike enough, surely, even to please you. And if, when he arrives,

my motives do not strike him in the true
light, you can readjust his thoughts to suit
yourself."

Miss Bolitho went out, and walked down
the drive that led to the village street.
The house that she left was of white rough-
cast, large and low. To one side of it rose
the mossy thatch roof of an enormous stone
barn, and into the court of which this barn
formed one side, an old oak gateway gave
entrance. The gateway had about it some
rude carving, which was almost falling to
pieces with age. On the other side of the
house was a high brick wall and the roofs
of smaller cottages; a little babbling stream
ran all the way across the small park
through which the drive made way. The
grass was rich under leafless elm trees, and
lusty daffodil clumps, among all the grass,
were gorgeous with yellow flowers.

It did not take more than ten minutes to
walk through the village, — a village of
rough-cast cottages and thatched roofs. A
quarter of a mile beyond the road bridged

the stream from the combe, which here
passed onward into level meadows.  On one
side, the hill rose high, and the way to
the moor was either over it or through the
combe.  Alice Bolitho, restless and eager
for a laborious walk, turned into the latter,
because she argued that if Mr. Knighton
had taken Harvey to his own house for
luncheon, — which appeared to her the
probable course, — they would after that
walk back to Norcombe House on a road
where the hillpath would be very visible.

The combe stream in the course of ages
had made a deep cutting, and on one side
the precipice was steep.  To the top of this
precipice the path ascended and ran on
halfway below the hilltop; the scrubby trees,
even the old gnarled roots, overhung the
path, and made it a concealed and secret
sort of place.  The length of this secluded
way was not so great as to make it an unusual country walk to any one accustomed to
such rambles; but when Alice had advanced
a certain distance and left the opening

almost halfway behind, she was surprised to
find that to-day the loneliness of the place
struck her with a dismal impression which
she had never derived from it before. She
remembered, too, that Knighton had told
her that he doubted the safety of the path,
but that was no sufficient reason for going
back; being warned, she could watch for a
broken place, and the bank above was not
so steep but that she could climb and pass
among the outgrowing trees. Why, then,
she asked herself, annoyed, did the recollec-
tion of this warning and the seclusion de-
press her? She was in the habit of walking
in this place and enjoying its gloom.

It is probable that when what is called a
presentiment is anything more than a curious coincidence, the law that governs it is
that of mind acting upon mind without the
ordinary medium of the senses. Alice Bolitho did not know of any danger that men-
aced, but some one else was at that moment
thinking upon it intently.

Alice had her dog with her — a golden

collie, in whose companionship she took the greatest delight. He was smiling now, as collies can smile, and bounding in front and bounding behind, barking with preposterous delight at the echo of his own voice. He was not depressed by any loneliness in the scene or fear of the narrow path; why should she be? She watched the path carefully to see that it was firm; she set the heel of her will, as it were, upon her unaccountable and unreasonable fear.

Quite unaccountable and unreasonable this fear — and yet where the precipice was high it suddenly sprang up before her, visible. A man crouching behind a wild holly-shrub rose with a cat-like spring. She swerved at the sight of him, but he had laid hold of her arm with an iron grasp.

She screamed. Her scream almost died on her lips, piercing only a little way into the air of the solitude around, falling again into a nervous moan, horrible to her own ears, so weak and hopeless was the sound. She screamed again, and again she knew that her voice had not carried beyond the trees of the lonely place. With all the strength that she possessed she tried without avail to wrench her arm from the grasp that held it. The stick in her hand was taken from her, and tossed like a child's plaything over the rocks into the stream below.

She called to her dog in breathless haste; she had enough voice, hoarse and unnatural as it sounded, to bid him spring upon her assailant. The dog, alas! had received no special training for the one accident of a lifetime. The man who had sprung from the trees wore no rags, nor did he smell like a beggar; the dog, eager to help his mistress in her obvious distress, decided that it was his most pleasing duty to seek the missing stick, and dashed away by a long détour to reach the foot of the precipice. Alice, unable at the moment to realize whither he had gone, only had this weird feeling added to her horrid plight, that the villain in whose violent hold she was had exercised

some mysterious repellent force by which
the dog had been terror-stricken.

The aspect of her enemy lent force to the
thought. He was not strong or brutal, as
one commonly thinks of brutal strength; he
was an old man, thin, white-haired, a face
and form in which it seemed as if mildness,
by some awful chemistry, had been changed
into a wolf-like ferocity.

"You are mad!" she exclaimed fiercely.

"Yes, young lady; mad — mad enough
for any extremity!"

"What do you want?"

For answer he began with sinewy strength
to press her forward to the edge of the
precipice.

It was only, perhaps, a hundred seconds
since he had first touched her, and now she
felt little hope, and believed that he would
cast her down upon the rocks beneath. The
shock, acting on a woman's weakness of
nerve, which until then she had never sus-
pected in herself, deprived her of physical
strength, almost of breath; and that her

mind did not fail, but grasped with steady clearness her whole situation, did not aid her — a delirium of fear or anger might have given back her strength.

"Listen, girl!" The man's eyes glared at her; she felt his hot breath with his words. "My son and I are hunted to death. We have taken refuge in a cellar of a mud hut on the heath yonder. My son is dying; he will never walk again in the light. Dying! Do you know what that means? No matter what he has done; they would catch him and drag him, dying as he is, into courts and prisons if they could. We are starving, starving! Do you know what that means?"

Quickly as the strenuous words were poured into her ear she began to understand. "I will give you money."

"Money, girl! I could give you more."

"I will give you food."

He began to speak again; his voice was slightly changed; his words did not come so terribly fast. At first she did not under-

stand at all; his subject seemed to have
changed; his words to be the utterance of
the wildest lunacy. Then, again, a light
came to her as to his meaning; he was
repeating an oath which he demanded that
she should repeat after him.

She was silent a minute longer, listening
to the words he poured upon her, her mind
terribly alive, her breath and pulses still
almost failing her. A promise extorted by
force need not, ought not, to be binding!
He would have her swear that she would
not convey to any human being the knowledge of himself or his hiding, that she
would bring to him food such as a sick man
might live upon, that she would conceal
what she did as if her own life depended
upon the concealment. The interests of law
and justice, the merest humanity to her
neighbors, demanded that such a promise
should be broken. The man was mad, and
therefore the threat of a horrible death
which his looks and actions pressed hard
upon her would, without this promise, be

fulfilled. The man was mad, and therefore words said to pacify him were as nothing.

"I swear to God " — whispered the man.

"I swear to God " — she repeated faintly.

"By His Son who loved us " — he continued.

And she went on repeating the words of the oath as he whispered them, like a child that lisped its first prayer.

Near the path the roots of bygone oaks held out queer arms and heads like gargoyles, and from these grew the young trees that held the canopy of dead leaves. Above was the quiet sky, around the silent hills, beneath the rocks and foaming stream. On the narrow ledge under the trees the old man and young woman stood almost quiet, the desperate antagonism of mind and will that was between them only showing in the fierce, nervous grasp by which he held her so perilously near the verge, and her pallid face and shrinking gesture.

"You think to break your oath," said the old man. He seemed to read, but without certainty, the thoughts in her mind. "You will say I compelled you; that you will not regard it!"

"I will keep the oath," she said, with white lips.

"Listen! Do you know what a soul is? The life that is you, that will live somewhere — think, act, live somehow, somewhere, for ever and ever and ever?" The fevered words sighed out over the rocky steep, and their whisper seemed to be echoed not by the rocks, but by the hissing movement of the sere leaves, "for ever and ever." "Can you think what it is to be a father, and have given such life to a son? to stand by and see that life hurled out of this mortal state, hurled on the downward track to a hell of evil deeds?" His mind dominated hers: she saw the vision he saw; it might be only a mad vision, not a reality, but she saw it. "Listen! You *keep* this word you have said, and I shall keep my son long enough to teach him a thing he needs to know, — a thing that will redeem his soul.

*I will teach him what love and mercy mean, and he will understand God's justice, and it will redeem his soul.* You *break* these words you have spoken, and " — His tones, now threatening, stopped; he looked wildly towards heaven.

Was he so mad, even now, when she had given the promise, as to think that her own soul would be more safe if hurried to instant death than if she had the chance to profane the vow?

His grasp upon her relaxed; he motioned her to the path with a gesture that told of gentle breeding, but it told also of trust reposed in her. It was just one moment more of his presence, but that moment of trust, too quickly gone to be arrested, appalled her more than the words she had said. Her mind, made up as to action, did not pause to know that this trust was appalling. She darted from her tormentor because she was free.

The dog, who, some forty feet below, had spent the time in excited movements upon the last accessible rock, trying to decide whether or not he would risk his life for the stick, now conveniently solved the problem by forgetting its existence, and incontinently raced back by the way he had come, making much scuffling with the earth and the dead bracken.    When he came past the spot of the encounter, the old man was going up the bank under the holly trees, and his mistress had gone on by the accustomed path; but so little notice did she take of him that he felt reproached in his mind, and remembered the stick, and went back once more to look at the whirling pool in which it lay.

Alice Bolitho ran upon the upward path. Her one thought was to find some one who would avenge her suffering and secure the enemy who was so mad and dangerous.

## CHAPTER III

THE laws which govern circumstance do not arrange the details of life to suit the lovers of a perfect tale. It might so easily have happened that one or both of the men who were chiefly interested in Alice Bolitho should have passed by, or just above, the place of her misadventure at the right time, and have heard her cry and rescued her; but, instead of that, Harvey and Knighton together had left the place long before she approached it, and Harvey, returning to it by himself, came just too late.

He had taken lunch at the inn, looked at the quaint little village, and glanced curiously through the gates at Norcombe House. After that he returned and established himself in the cottage upon the hill, and strolled again to the spot whose beauty had so fascinated him — the upper entrance to the combe.

The path here was a descending ledge, and the side of the hill curved in and out with the winding of the stream below. Descending a little way, Harvey was standing above the path among the trees, and was feeling rather than observing the prospect before him, when suddenly in the stillness of the place he heard a light footfall coming up with speed. As he looked, a girl came round the turning into view. Her face was very white; indeed, it appeared to Harvey to be so blanched of all color that he did not truly know for a moment whether he looked at a woman or at a ghost — if a ghost could sustain the weight of ordinary clothing.

As for the girl, when she caught sight of him she hesitated, first, as it seemed, with an impulse of renewed terror, and next, apparently, with an eager desire to speak. So astonished he was, he stood still, leaning perforce, as he had been, against a tree to keep his footing, and the girl, as these changes of impulse passed over her, stood upon the path looking up to him. It proved, however, that the white lips formed no word, that there was no voice to come from the throat of this pallid creature. A few moments more, and she had gone on as she came, running with light fleet step up to the moor.

Harvey followed, but at a more reasonable pace, for when her back was turned the ordinary habits of life so far reasserted themselves as to remind him that to run upon the heels of a young lady would not tend to lessen her fears if she were afraid, and in any case was a proceeding too odd to be justified by the mere sight of a sheet-like countenance.

When he reached the open, he still saw the figure which had recently been near him. She was traveling upon the upper path in the Norcombe direction, and as he followed, returning to his rooms, he still saw her in advance, until she went over the hill where it dipped suddenly to the village.

Twilight crept gray and silent over the

moor.  Harvey realized that he had come
to sojourn in the world's most quiet corner.

After dinner he met Knighton by appointment at Norcombe Inn, whence they
were both to repair to Miss Bolitho's drawing-room for that first interview, so terri-
fying and at the same time so interesting
to Harvey.  Harvey had, however, now a
counteracting subject of interest.

"I never saw any one look in more of a
funk," he said to Knighton, after having
related the incident.

"Most extraordinary!  What did she
wear?"

"Have n't the slightest idea."

"Well, I mean was she a gentlewoman?"

"Yes, certainly that."

They were walking together in the dusky
night towards Norcombe House.  Knighton's questions came sharply, with pauses
for reflection between.

"Was she thin — in a black dress?"

"No."

A longer pause; then Knighton said, in
a voice that had a studied effort of calm: —

"It must have been Miss Bolitho. She is the last person I would have expected to be frightened in the way you describe, unless there was very sufficient cause, which I trust there was not."

Knighton was tramping along at a great rate as he spoke. If Harvey had been more at leisure from himself, he would have observed that the motive power of this swift walking was inward perturbation; but he observed nothing, his mind was full of the idea that possibly he had already seen his lady-love, and he was trying to recall more particularly what she was like.

The night was not dark; the stream running in the grass of the park was just apparent as they passed over. Through the leafless twigs of high trees the stars were shining. In the lower windows of the square white house there was light.

"But who," said Harvey, "is the thin person you mentioned, with the black dress?"

"You did not suppose that Miss Bolitho lived here all alone?"

"I never thought anything about it."

"Mrs. Ross, a young widow who is a distant relative, is staying with her."

"Both young! Are they attached to one another?"

"Miss Bolitho has an affection for Mrs. Ross which is to me rather unaccountable, for I should not fancy Mrs. Ross to be very congenial."

When they entered the house they were shown into a square sitting-room on the lower floor; oak beams crossed and recrossed each other in the low ceiling, the three windows opening on the park were low and square, all the furniture was dark and plain. At a square table the ladies sat with their work, and they both rose, coming forward a pace or two, and at first sight Harvey was sorry that he had been told that the thin lady in black was not Alice Bolitho, for she was fairer to look at than the other. On either side of a pretty face light, waving hair was brushed with nun-like simplicity; her very delicacy gave grace to her figure;

if she was pale, the excitement of their
entrance had brought a rose-flush to her
cheeks; if she was older than her companion, she hardly looked it in the lamplight.
Miss Bolitho, on the other hand, was a
much more ordinary-looking person; she
had an appearance of sturdy strength; her
face, though fresh and pleasing, was not at
all beautiful; her dark abundant hair was
arranged with no attempt to make it appear
either æsthetic or fashionable. Harvey distinctly felt that the stars in their courses
might have been more favorable to him.

The shaded lamp did not allow him to be
sure at the first greeting whether or not he
had seen Alice Bolitho before. He sat a
little back from the table, endeavoring to
observe her face more carefully.

The conversation went lamely, for Knighton appeared to have the grim idea that
Harvey, having been introduced, should now
shine in the talk with uneclipsed light, and
Mrs. Ross, with a pretty air of shy deference, looked to Miss Bolitho to answer all

the remarks that either of the men made. Harvey anathematized Knighton as a tact-less fool, but it did not occur to him to make the same criticism upon the lady with the pretty face.    At last he said: —

"I think I cannot be mistaken — I think I saw you to-day coming up the combe."

"Yes; I was just thinking it must have been you whom I saw there."

Ever since they had come in, Miss Bolitho had been replying with quiet, candid good sense.    Harvey thought she would have been more attractive if she had shown the sensibility of the embarrassing nature of the occasion which her companion was display-ing; and that she should also propose to treat their meeting of the afternoon as if nothing remarkable had characterized it, appeared to him distinctly cold and artifi-cial.    Now that he saw her in abundant health and calm of nerve, what he had wit-nessed in the afternoon appeared more and more extraordinary.    Knighton, who was at this point fidgeting almost noisily with

his chair, made an apparent effort to say
nothing.

Harvey smiled across the table to his
cousin.

"You surely were feeling faint or frightened when I saw you. I — I almost
thought — almost thought you were a spir-
itual creature, you were so pale."

"Yes; I was feeling faint and very much
frightened."

"Oh, Alice, my dear, how was it that
you did not tell me? Feeling faint and
frightened, and you were alone!" The
words were uttered in a voice full of feeling. Mrs. Ross had come out of herself, it
appeared, in her distress about the revelation just made.

Alice replied, with just the slightest touch
of irritation in her voice, "The faintness
was over in a minute, Amy; it was not
worth mentioning."

"Oh, my dear," with great affection,
"to think that you should have been faint
— you who are so strong! If it had been

me, now, it would have been nothing, not to be considered for a moment."

Alice was silent.

"What frightened you?" This question came from Knighton, in a voice low and determined, and Alice looked across at him a moment with clear, kindly eyes before she answered. It seemed to rest her so to look and meet his gaze; but Harvey was not observing her, he was noticing Amy Ross, who was brooding over the rebuff of Alice's silence. She had drawn her chair a little farther from the light; there was a look of pain and patience in her delicate face, and something that suggested that that look was frequently to be seen there.

"I walked through the combe," said Alice. "You told me not to go" (this to Knighton), "but I thought that, being warned that the path might be loose, I was safe enough. Yet for some reason, when I got to " — (her voice faltered, it was a moment before she could go on) — "to the ledge over the rock — I became quite dizzy and frightened. I did not know before that I could be so foolish and weak."

"What frightened you?" Knighton repeated his question with exactly the same force.

Alice smiled. "You know," in an explanatory tone, "I am not the least superstitious. I don't believe that people with pale faces may be ghosts as likely as not" (she glanced mockingly at Harvey), "yet I confess that I had a fit of nerves, or a presentiment of evil, or whatever you may call it, that I can't account for, and when I got to the steepest place I was terrified; I was only too glad to run up to the moor as quickly as I could."

"You could not have run uphill if you were faint," said Knighton.

"It was when I stopped for a bit that I felt faint."

"Do you mean me to understand that this terror came upon you without your seeing or hearing anything to cause it?" Knighton asked this sternly.

There was just an instant's pause. Then Alice answered evasively, "Yes, that is what I wish you to understand."

When the men were gone, the two women within the house went to their sleeping-rooms.

Amy Ross, upon shutting her own door, fell into a little reverie before her toilet-glass. She was afraid of Knighton — that is, she thought he disapproved of her, and she always feared disapproval; but she decided that she liked the newcomer. She began to think what this and that expression on his face had meant. After a little reflection, she could have given an account of all his inward thoughts and feelings during the evening. Then she remembered how very happy he and Alice would probably be together; the remembrance saddened her, and naturally, because there was no place for herself in the vision. There are few of us who are unselfish enough to enjoy festivities of heart from which our hearts are shut out. Then she recollected that she would for the present have the interesting occupation of guiding the course of true love in the right channel; that, as she loved to be of use, put heart into her again.

When Alice Bolitho entered her bedroom she did not linger in pensive meditation; she did what she had to do with ordinary rapidity, and that was to go to bed. The room was chilly, for one thing (Amy had a fire, but she had none); for another, she longed to have the candle out; she hated the very sight of herself that evening. Yet when her head was pillowed in the darkness she did not for a long time even think of sleep.

With hands clasped under her thick tresses, and head that lay outwardly quiet upon the hands, and eyes wide open to the darkness, the girl lay looking into the situation in which she found herself.

It was hard, hard indeed, that among all the women of her class in peaceful England, who passed their lives in unruffled security, she should have been one of the very few to be molested by a violent hand. She was sure that statistics would show that the chances against any real danger on a country road were so great that to have seriously listened to her curious preliminary fears would have been quite foolish, yet the event had proved most miserable.

Miserable in this, — that the adventure, short and barren of such horrors as any imagination might conjure up, had, just by its reality, struck down her strength, physical and moral, with such an easy blow; and in this also, that the trap which had been laid for her was a worn-out, rusty thing. It seemed to her excited brain as if many of the pages of romance were soiled with vows of help and concealment weakly taken under the compulsion of fear.

It was a most amazing thing that two criminals, or, rather, one dying criminal and his protector, should have taken refuge in so quiet a neighborhood, and should claim from her, the only woman of substance near, that she should feed them and keep their secret till death came for the younger man. More extraordinary did this seem because she now believed that the thin aged creature who had extorted this promise from her was a man of gentle birth and life, and not more mad than every man may be in his direst extremity.

It was plainly not for the good of society that this man or any other should be able to rely upon a promise compelled by force. It was not the best thing for the community in which she lived that such desperate characters should remain hidden there. It was worse for the men themselves, one aged, the other dying, to suffer want and exposure than to be placed in some prison hospital. It was plainly a most disagreeable course for herself, to keep such a secret, to prevaricate and evade the questions of her best friends, and to afford the constant help to these men that would be necessary.

As well as Alice could spell out the dictate of common sense, it bade her notify the authorities, in the person of Mr. Knighton, that men were starving in one of the cottages on the moor, but was there not a stronger command than this?

One consideration, as it appeared to Alice, was stronger, and that was the intensely disagreeable feeling of dishonor that overcame her when she had actually essayed to take the course that wisdom indicated. Out of cowardice she had given a promise, and given it in words of which the very remembrance sapped all her self-respect; she had vowed, and she had deliberately repeated the vow, and now to break it seemed such a low and bad thing to do that she must be *sure* that there was harm in keeping it before she broke it.

Alice Bolitho looked into the darkness, and as clear to her mind as it had been to her eyes some hours before when she had made a visit in the dusk, rose the picture of the interior of a broken cottage, of a young man in the last stages of wasting disease, and of the old man, weak with the reaction from his fierce assault, trembling with the palsy of starvation. These men could not injure others, she thought; the harm would be to themselves, and the counterbalancing good the old man looked for was a matter of circumstances and beliefs of which she knew nothing. "Well," she sighed, "that is his responsibility." And the harm would be to herself. She felt that for her cowardice she deserved discomfort, and she plainly chose the least discomfort in keeping her word rather than in breaking it.

This was the way the thoughts of Alice Bolitho ran on the evening of the day on which she had first seen her suitor. Once she thought of him. "Oh, I wish," she said to herself, "that I could tell him all about it; he looks as if he would be kind, but of course he could n't take the responsibility of keeping the thing quiet." After a moment she added, "Neither could Mr. Knighton."

## CHAPTER IV

THE next day was Saturday. It was brighter weather; the yellow sunshine was pouring down upon the desolate combe and upon the haze of buds that began to rest on all the trees of the Norcombe meadows. Harvey's picture needed a gray light, so he could not begin it; and moreover, picture or no picture, he had no intention of wasting any time before making friends with Alice Bolitho. He was not so much frightened at her now. He found himself again in the low square sitting-room at the homely hour of two. Amy Ross was there, but she was not the person with whom it was his business to make friends.

"Will you come out into the sunshine and show me the place?" he asked Alice.

She took her hat from a peg in the hall, put it on without consulting a looking-glass,

and, dragging on a jacket somewhat awk-
wardly as she walked, she led the way down
a mossy path to a garden inclosed by the
old brick wall.

It seemed that she did a great deal of her
own gardening. She was entirely interested
in hotbeds and cold-frames, and the plants
in a few small glass houses. There were
not many flowers; there were a great many
young vegetables and fruit plants to be
looked at, and when occasion required she
shifted the glass frames herself, without
thinking of waiting for him to do it.

Harvey was not much interested in the
plants, but on the whole he grew more and
more pleased with his companion. The clear
gray eyes, with their dark brows and lashes,
the clear skin that flushed with exercise,
and the thick, dark, glossy hair, gave come-
liness to features that, if too broad and
immobile for beauty, were tolerably well
formed. And then there was this great
charm, — the charm of possession, or almost
possession. Harvey had never felt in any

way bound by relationship to a young woman before. This Alice had a quiet, good-
natured way of talking familiarly to him,
as if kindliness were a matter of course.
The sun shone warmly, the birds twittered
on every side, there was a feeling as of
growing green in the air. When they left
the garden and were walking farther down
the park, they came upon an old bench,
and there he announced his desire to sit for
a while.

"Well, you sit there, and I 'll sit on the
dyke," said Alice.

It was a low stone dyke, and she lifted
herself to the top of it with ease. There
were soft guttural sounds to be heard on
the other side of it.

"But why will you not sit on the bench?
It is much more comfortable."

"For two reasons" (her smile was perfectly frank). "In the first place, I want
to look over at my pigs — No, that is not
the *first ;* the other reason is the more important, and that is, that Amy is in the sitting-

room and cannot fail to see us out of the window."

"But for you and me there can be no reason in that." He made the assertion with joyous confidence.

"Oh, for you and me, or for you and any one else, or for me and any one else, there is no reason in it at all, except that dear little Amy is always in quest of emotion and romance and excitement, and such people are apt to find what they look for, especially when it is n't there."

"She seems to be warm-hearted."

"She has lots of feelings of every sort; and there is another fine feature in her character: that is her little boy, who comes for his holidays; he is a darling."

In a minute she spoke again.

"I don't understand how you can hear those fascinating gruntings and not want to look over and see my pigs. I am very fond of pigs, and I have them washed; in poor grandpa's time they did not smell nice."

"I am so much interested in something else, Alice. May I call you Alice?"

"If you like."

"And you will call me Hal?"

"If you like."

He had a sense that he was becoming absurd. "Well, but look here, we ought to be frank with one another and come to some understanding, you know. Your grandfather urgently requested us to marry one another, unless there was some good reason against it, and I suppose we ought, don't you?"

"I suppose we owe it to him to try to like one another," she replied. She was looking over at the pigs.

"If you don't see any objection to his plan at present, we will assume that there is none until it turns up."

"At present it is a merely provisional friendship," she said.

He sat silent for a good while. It was a place where silence was delightful. The pigs seemed to have gone to sleep; the yellow, misty sunlight cast the shadow of the trees upon stone and brick, and upon the grass of the park where the daffodils grew.

After that they went to a field where the newest and smallest lambs were to be seen. They were very well-bred lambs, and she explained to him their pedigree. They made the circuit of the place, patting the cow and the pony and the dog. It was, take it altogether, a humble ménage, but to Alice each animal had so strong a personality that to have expressed a desire that they should be finer or more numerous would have seemed like expressing the same desire to a proud mother exhibiting her little family.

"To-morrow is Sunday," said Harvey. "May I come and go to church with you?"

"I never go to church; from my point of view there is no reason why I should go."

"I can't help being sorry for that; but since it is so, may I come and spend the time to-morrow morning with you?"

"If you see any reason for going to church, no reason should be sufficient to keep you from it, and I shall not be at home."

Just here she seemed to lapse into serious thoughts of her own. He had only seen this girl twice, and had not been with her very long either time, and yet this was not the first time that he had been conscious that her attention had wandered completely from him, and in these fits of absence she looked absorbed, almost dejected. This did not seem to him an amiable feature in her manner when he came to think it over; it almost counter-balanced the good-natured readiness with which she accepted him as a friend.

Sunday was gray and stormy, just the light and the wild effect that he wanted for his picture. He was afraid that Alice would despise him if he did not go to church. "People who are not religious expect so much of people who are," he said to himself petulantly. This was when he had risen early to inspect the weather. As if in answer came the sound of the Norcombe church - bell ringing for an eight o'clock service. He bethought him that it would do to go now and not later, so he ran down and said some prayers in a back seat.

There were only a handful of people in the church. One of them was Mrs. Ross. She looked forlorn in the early light, and he could not help noticing that, as she knelt with her face covered, she wept nearly all the time of the service. It was impossible to help being sorry for her; probably she mourned her dead husband.

He sauntered out, and met the object of his sympathy in the churchyard. She turned her face away from him as they walked together, in order to hide the traces of her tears. He could only speak of the weather and ask how Alice was.

"I do not think she is quite well; she has not been herself since you came; but that is natural, and I am glad to see it. You do not know what a fine girl she is, what a beautiful character."

"I am learning to know."

"Ah, yes; but there is so much to learn of her excellence, it will take you a long

time. Indeed, I mean just what I say.
Oh, she is strong! She is fine! I am such
a weak character myself; I cannot sufficiently admire her."

"Your warm praise speaks also for your
own generosity."

"I am not generous, I am only just; indeed, do you know, I sometimes almost suspect myself of a little jealousy towards her
— a very little, you know; or, no, I do not
think it can be that, because I love her: it
is only that I feel that my happiness " (her
voice fell very low) "is past and hers is to
come. Do you think that that is jealousy?"

"No" (warmly); "I am sure that no one
could speak as you have just spoken who
was jealous."

In a minute he added, "I am sorry you
think that Alice has been agitated since I
came." He was not exactly sorry, but it
was an interesting revelation, and he wanted
to hear more of it.

"Yes, decidedly. I have known her all
her life, but I have never seen her so much

agitated. I am sure her heart is stirred to the depth. She has at times looked very sad, very pale, and once, when she did not know I saw her, she gave a gesture almost as if of wild distress."

"I cannot be expected to be pleased to hear this" (in some chagrin).

"Oh, yes" (hastily). "I would not have told you if I had not been sure that you should gain the greatest hope from it. You know, I am older than both of you, and I have seen so much, passed through so much. Oh, with Alice, believe me, nothing could be so cheering! Her life has hitherto been so passionless; it has been smooth, like a placid, sunny river; and now she feels that that old unemotional self is passing from her, she loses something which she has had always, and goes forward into the unknown. She would not be a woman if she did not tremble for the future and shed some tears for the past."

"I am glad you think that," he said; "it seemed to me that if — if I might say that

Alice had a fault (it cannot be treason to speak of it to one who loves her so much), that she was a little indifferent, a little unfeeling, if that is not too strong a word."

"Self-poised, perhaps" (as if correcting his expression). "Yes, dear Alice! — But that, you see, is just what is breaking up, may I say, at the kiss of the fairy prince."

Harvey felt soothed and pleased with Amy's view of his standing with Alice. Amy might have a slight tendency to exaggerate and gush, but she had nice feelings. They separated where their roads parted, and Harvey went up to his breakfast.

The day grew colder and the wind more strong; Harvey realized that he could not work at his easel outside. He had no thought on that account of giving up; he set up his canvas within, and went out to imprint the scene upon his memory.

He went out for this purpose the first time at ten o'clock, went back and worked for some twenty minutes, went out again to correct his impression, went back and cor-

rected his outline, and a third time stood in
the upper opening of the combe, only his
powers of observation at work, the rest of
him quiescent.

It was then that Alice Bolitho passed
him the second time, coming up the combe
path with a pale face and hunted look.   In-
cidents never repeat themselves.   This time
the girl was by no means so pale as before,
and she had no appearance of indecision, —
quite the contrary.   Harvey was much farther back among the trees than before.
Alice did not see him, but went steadily on
up the path.

Harvey did not know why her face had
restrained him from calling her name; he
did not know, when he reviewed it, why the
circumstance in the first minute had shocked
him as it did.   There was nothing very
remarkable in a girl of Alice's character
walking again through a place in which she
had felt the disagreeable sensations of ver-
tigo and alarm, just as she would have rid-
den a shying horse up to the object from

which it had shied.  He did not think she
was wise in doing so; he ran down the
combe path at once to see the ledge over the
cliff and decide for himself if it were safe.

When he had run about three hundred
yards, he could command a view of all the
narrow bit of the path and of the cliff beneath.  The path would certainly be the
better for a railing.  It was a pretty hillpath, but not a safe one for a girl who had
felt her head swim.

As he looked, the dead oak leaves shiv-
ered and hissed in the wind.  The oaks
were still in winter, almost budless, but the
bank, covered with mossy roots and patches
of fern, was green, and the lower precipice
of sheer rock, with the stream foaming at
its base, pleased his eye.  Harvey took in
all the lonely beauty of the place and went
back again.

He was just in time to see Alice disappear over a rise of the moor, going towards
the old cottages, whose chimneys he could
barely see.

Harvey did not think of following her,
remembering that she had refused his prof-
fered company for that morning.  He went
on with his work, and so grateful was the
moorland air, and so lovely the greens and
browns of the quiet hills, that he did not
wonder that she loved to range in the open
alone.

In the meantime, Alice, unconscious that
she had been seen, approached the hovels in
the hollow.  As she appeared at one side
she saw old Gor deliberately turn and hobble away in an opposite direction.  From
this she felt convinced that the old witch
knew that she had neighbors, and that for
the sake of gold or other consideration she
would see or hear nothing the witnessing of
which might bring her or others into trouble.  Alice looked at the old woman's un-
easy gait, trying to estimate how safe soup
or milk would be in her custody.  She
would have been glad indeed to have found
a messenger she might employ if the weary
work she had undertaken was to go on.

She stopped at a hut whose bulging wall and loosened roof made it appear more empty and desolate even than its neighbors, and, calling to the unseen inmates from outside the door, she waited until it was opened. The windows were obscured; rubbish that had collected upon the threshold had not been removed, but the door, which opened inwards, revealed a part of the cottage, a mere cell, that was dry and wholesome enough. It was here the sick man's bed had been made. The old man, white, fragile, stood holding the door to speak with her.

Alice gave one swift glance through to the bed and then stepped back, preferring to stand where she could not see the shining eyes of woe and pain that looked at her therefrom. She set down a bottle of liquid upon the doorstep.

"I ask you again to release me from this promise!" She spoke to the old man, and, involuntarily even, she lowered her voice so that the piteous creature within might be spared the hearing of her words.

The aged father closed the door behind him, and seemed to cower upon the threshold as he held up clasped hands before her. The gesture was the natural body of his prayer, no external clothing that would have robbed it of all strength in her eyes. The fierce passion of his one desire rendered all that he did simple, and there was about him a venerableness and gentility that made his agony touching to her, although hateful for that very cause.

Involuntarily she turned away.

"What can you gain by this?" she asked again in a minute. "Your son should have a doctor, you know."

He was holding himself within the lintel of the door. She was under the impression that he told her that the doctors had already given up the case as hopeless, but she did not listen accurately to the words, she was trying to form another argument.

"I don't believe," she said, "that any change that could take place in his mind now would make any difference to his religion." She was trying to argue from the point of view of one who held that conversion at a former period would have been desirable.

In a moment she perceived that she had said carelessly, roughly, words that gave more pain than if to some sanguine heart she had casually expressed the belief that a loved person was about to die; and she saw now that the father, who quailed and shuddered at her words, had his own fear to fight against when he still hoped to the end for the thing which he was striving to bring about.

"Nay, but for the sake of pity let me try!" he whispered, and there was a catch in his breath as if some inward prayer, constantly repeated, had interrupted the outward words; the inward breathing, "God have mercy!" was half audible.

In pity she spoke more gently. "But I don't understand. You said that to teach him what love and mercy are would convert him; but if you believe that God is love and mercy, why do you suppose that He will judge your son more hardly than you do?"

"You are young; you have not known sin. I have no words, but my heart knows what the boy needs. Listen! Don't you see that there is law, there is justice, in love; but to the boy in there justice looks like injustice, because he does not know that he has sinned. Don't you see that it is only when he knows what mercy is that he can know that he has wronged it, and it is only when he knows that he is wrong that he can begin to be right? Ah, young lady, you little know the unbelief and evil abroad now in the world; but there are men with heads astray, and they think"— Words seemed to fail him; his voice shook with excitement and his head with weakness; the wind tossed his thin, white hair and beard.

Alice wondered if he was really very old, or if age and whiteness of hair had not come upon him suddenly in the last few weeks.

"They think," whispered the trembling voice excitedly, "that when they do the

devil's work there is no sin against God in
it. Ah me! it was not until my boy saw
that his life was my life, and his wretchedness my wretchedness, that he saw that he
had done wrong to me. You don't know
it; I never knew it until my boy's soul
came to hang upon it; but remember it
now, lady, because I tell you that *it is only
by knowing that there is nothing but mercy
in God's heart that we see the justice of
hell.* You do not know what I mean. No,
no; I seem to you as one mad; but give me
time, give me time to influence my son, and
may God, who will certainly requite you in
blessing, have mercy on us." He groped
his way inside the door again, and shut it
gently.

Alice went slowly away — not back as
she had come, but to reach another road that
crossed the hill. Her mind was as little at
peace with itself as it had been in the first
hour of this adventure; she did not truly
know what course she ought to take. The
fact that the thing which the old father

aimed at was in her mind shadow, not substance, did not alter in the least her pity
for his desire, or her merciful wish that he
might suppose it to be gratified. Nor did
the knowledge that the younger man was a
criminal make it appear less desirable to
assuage his evident suffering by every possible means. She had been told that the
police were hunting for him; she had no
doubt that, fanaticism and the prejudice
against being arrested apart, the best thing
that could befall him would be that they
should find him; but then a man is what
his hopes and fears, longings and beliefs
are, and not to be considered apart from
them. It is that which makes dealings
with real men so different from any nice
adjustment of theories concerning such dealings. Alice Bolitho did not say this to
herself clearly, but she summed it up in
thinking of her ineffectual attempt to reason
with the old man.

"He is simply the most impossible person
I ever came across," she said to herself.

## CHAPTER V

THAT evening Harvey walked over to call on Mr. Knighton. Knighton was quite the principal man of the neighborhood. Alice described him as very rich and very grand and accustomed to order everybody about. It was, as it were, the habit of generations that the Knightons should be kind to the Bolithos, and take charge of their welfare to a certain extent. Harvey had come in for his share of this tacit patronage, and his present call was a necessary acknowledgment. It did not occur to him to inquire whether he liked Knighton or not; Knighton was a man whom every one trusted and admired, and who was not supposed to crave such a flimsy sentiment as liking.

The highroad that lay at the foot of the hill led to Knighton Hall. The master was found in his library. It was a large room,

containing an immense number of books.
The light was not at all adequate to the
room; it consisted of one immense candle
hooded with a student's reflector. Knighton
pushed up the reflector out of deference to
his guest, and the result was a sort of Rem-
brandt effect, by which one spot in the room
appeared very bright in comparison to the
graduating darkness on all sides. In the
bright spot was Knighton's face and figure,
and Harvey thought what a fine old fellow
he was growing to be, and wondered if he
himself would be as old and as fixed in his
ways at fifty. "Squires still retain full
dignity in this out-of-the-way corner of the
world," he said to himself. "I had thought
that as a body they had marched into the
past, and only lived in the pages of unorigi-
nal romance."

"You have seen Miss Bolitho again?"
Knighton asked with the magisterial air of
one whose business it was to inquire.

"Yes." Harvey beamed with satisfaction. "I spent yesterday afternoon with

her. I think we are going to get on together."

Knighton looked upon him indulgently;
his elation betrayed what his diffidence had
been.

"I saw her again to-day," said Harvey.
He hesitated. Then he told that Alice had
passed him in the morning.

"You think that she went just because
she wished to overcome her nervousness of
last Friday?"

Harvey had expressed some suggestion of
this sort, but now replied, "I cannot tell at
all; you know her and the place better than
I do."

Knighton tapped his table with impatience. He was saying to himself that there
had been more in Alice's alarm of Friday
than she was willing to tell, but he saw no
reason for mentioning this to Harvey.

Harvey did not stay late, and when he
left, Knighton, whose activity seemed un-
bounded, walked with him towards Norcombe for exercise. They had much talk

together, for Harvey felt that it was his
business to inform himself about the country he was in, and he could not have met
with any one more able to give exhaustive
information on every point, from the history
of the neighborhood since the time of the
Romans to the most modern methods of till-
ing the land.   If Harvey had not been intelligent he would have been weary; to his
credit be it said that he eagerly drank in
instruction.

"It is one of the few localities left in
England that can truly be said to be un-
frequented as yet," Knighton was saying.
"If the New Zealander does not come pretty
soon to stand on the ruins of London Bridge,
the Land's End will, of course, become a
suburb, a newer Kensington; but at present we are in peace.   There are not half
a dozen cottages within a radius of ten miles
that let lodgings; most of our people never
sent or received a telegram, and have never
heard of electric lights."

"You think that the old ways are better;

you think that it is a salvation, in sort, to
the present generation to be preserved from
this?"

"I would not be so rash as to form such
an opinion; it is impossible for me to say
that the rush of modern inventions is not
the herald of the kingdom of light, or to
tell whether the average standard of moral-
ity and godliness will be in any way " —

Knighton's voice suddenly stopped.
What Harvey noticed about the stoppage
was that the speaker did not seem conscious
that it was obvious. In a few moments he
pronounced the next word as if he had not
been surprised by something in the meantime.

— "affected by these things," he concluded.

To the left of their road lay low meadows;
to the right the hill rose with fine precipitous sides. The moon was seen among
breaking clouds in the eastern sky, and by
its light even Harvey, inexperienced in the
landmarks, could perceive that they were

approaching Norcombe, and that a few minutes' walk would bring them to the place
where his own path ascended from the road.
Two women were walking a little in front
of them; except for that, there was no one
to be seen.

"It is hard to connect any poetical idea
with a future of electric machines," said
Harvey; "and it is trite to say that that
which cannot belong to true poetry must be
diabolical; the thing that is holy *must* be
beautiful."

If Knighton was absorbed, as Harvey
had half a notion that he was, in recog-
nizing the two women in front of him, he
might have easily let this remark pass without immediate answer, but instead of that,
he answered it hastily: —

"By the time the moss on all our by-roads
is trodden away, some better form of beauty
than moss may be given us; it is not for us
to judge; a man is a fool who forms an
opinion without knowing all the facts."

It seemed to Harvey that he was speak-

ing a little louder and walking a little
faster. They passed the two women. Here
for a moment there was something slightly
distraught in Knighton's hesitation again;
and then he went on for some five minutes
explaining that the future was unknown,
and the past and present only imperfectly
known, hence— But they had got to the
point now where Harvey must ascend the
hill, and Knighton, who was not a man to
dally even for talk, abruptly postponed the
argument.

"You are returning?" said Harvey.

"No, not till I have walked through Norcombe to see that the place is in order; it
is my regular length of walk when I come
in this direction. Good-night."

"He is quite like the pious Califs of
Eastern tales," commented Harvey, toiling
up the steep. "I am sure he thought those
women were out too late, and will call at
their cottages to-morrow to read them a
lecture."

In the meantime Knighton, walking on

towards Norcombe, slackened his pace. His whole attention was given to the footsteps coming behind him, but he did not look round; he passed over the bridge at the opening of the combe, and the women passed over just behind him. The wind came in long miserable moans down the opening; the stream bubbled underneath the long bridge where it began to spread out into the meadow. Knighton hesitated, uncertain whether the women were following, until they were close upon him; then he went on, and the women behind him until they turned up a lane that led past Miss Bolitho's stables. After that Knighton finished his walk at his usual quick pace.

Next morning Alice Bolitho was sowing flower-seeds in a hotbed within the brick-walled garden. She was kneeling on a wooden board, and her garden gloves were lying beside her. The sun was warm within those sheltering walls; a robin was hopping not far from her, expecting, no doubt, that she would take the gardener's spade and begin to dig and throw up some worms. Alice did not even notice the robin; she was intent on letting drop little even trails of seed up and down the scratches she had made in the black mould contained in the frame. A shadow fell across her work. She looked up to see Knighton looking down at her with concern and curiosity.

"Well now, what is all this about?" asked he. He spoke in a low, wheedling tone. After a minute he said, "Was it Mary you had with you last night?"

Alice still knelt. She was looking down at her seeds now, but she was doing nothing. "Yes, it was Mary."

"I suppose the wench, ill-tempered as she is, would do anything you coaxed her into. Who was ill in our direction that you thought you ought to visit them at that time of night?" Knighton continued to look searchingly at the young gardener; she was not looking at him. "What did you walk up the combe again for yesterday morning when you thought we all were in church?"

"What do you know about that?"

He told her all that he knew.

"Did Hal Harvey recognize me last night?"

"No; and as you did not choose to speak to us, I supposed you wished to be left alone."

"Then don't tell him now."

"Why not?"

"Because I ask it."

"A sufficient reason, Alice" (he lingered on her name a moment); "but now tell me" —

"I cannot."

"Why not?"

"I cannot even tell you why I cannot; I can tell you nothing."

His face and attitude expressed one quality, perhaps the least to be expected of him just then, that was patience.

"Have we gone back into the middle ages, or are we living in a novel?" (A full minute passed in silence.) "At the third volume, towards the end?" he suggested with irony.

"I wish it may be very near the end."

Knighton waited a minute or two longer, but silence from her forced him into speech. "Well, what am I to make of this? I have lived at Norcombe for nearly half a century, and I never knew anything happen in it that was not absolutely humdrum. I have known you for — let me see, is it twenty-four years? — since I used to ride by and see you, as pink as a little piggy, wrapped in dimity and trundled in a bauble-coach; and I have never known you do anything that was not moderately wise and good, and now — you are terror-struck in lonely places and will not tell what alarms you; you go out at night alone; you have begun to behave altogether in a reprehensible, I might say suspicious, way, and will give me no explanation of it. You even imply by your last words that the course of conduct on which you have entered is not yet ended. Your grandfather is dead; your father and mother are dead; and I, who have been their friend and am yours — what am I to do? Shall I send a cohort of my men over to guard the lonely roads in the daytime and to guard your house at night, with orders not to let you pass? or shall I turn detective and escort in one, as I did last night, and spend my time watching you?"

"Do you think it is necessary to watch me?"

"I am asking you what you would do in my place?"

"I would say to myself, ' I have questioned her, and she will not explain; I have commanded, and she will not obey; I have warned her, and I am not justified in any further interference.' "

"Not justified," he repeated slowly (there was a ring of sadness in the word); "but would Harvey be justified? and in that case is it not my duty to appeal to him?"

She lifted her head with a fierce gesture. "What could he do? If *he* attempted to interfere with me in any way, I should bid him leave Norcombe to-morrow."

Knighton stood considering. He could

not do what would cause a rupture between these new friends.

"I cannot even imagine what you were at, Alice. If you had not just confessed that you had a secret, I would hope that the matter was trivial; but I have not even that consolation now. If you were that pretty little widow in the house yonder, I would think that you had got up a mystery for the sake of satisfying your own craving for some new sensation." (He stopped abruptly, and took a pace or two on the garden path.) "Without any clue, how am I to advise, how am I to protect you?"

He had confronted her again, and she had risen to stand before him.

"I do not think I need protection," she said. "I *think*" (there was some honest dubiety in her tone) "that I have been and shall be safe. I know that I must appear to you silly and headstrong. I am very sorry, but I cannot help it. I have just one thing to ask, Mr. Knighton."

"Well, out with it."

"If you meet me again, do not look at me; do not look at what I do or where I go."

"Are you serious? You ask a hard thing!"

"I can only ask; the rest must lie with you."

In Knighton the instinct of curiosity was by no means dominant, yet, as he turned in impatience to pace down a line of planks that were laid for a foot-walk upon a muddy path, he was unconscious of his own movement or where he set his feet; he was wholly absorbed in the questions of his curiosity. Had Alice got into some entanglement in her school or college days, of which she was now reaping some bitter result? Or was it merely that some friend, male or female, had turned up in the neighborhood, and applied to her for secret help, or — several other questions of like nature flashed into a mind not usually fertile in extraordinary surmises; but the mind was wholly just in this, that, having no reason to know, it did not allow itself to conjecture. He turned and came back along the board walk, and found her standing just where he left her.

"You are not an ignorant miss; you know the world as well as a man of your age ought to know it; I suppose" — reluctantly — "I can trust you to take care of yourself."

Having said this, he went away with as little greeting as when he came.

## CHAPTER VI

IT was that day that Harvey told Alice about the picture he had begun.

"I can't think you are wise," she said, "to have taken the first picturesque bit you saw without waiting to choose. Why, I could drive you in one afternoon to half a dozen more worthy subjects. This shows me how little you know of our beauties."

"But, you know, one *feels* a subject for a picture. I do not choose it, it chooses me; and this place claimed me at once. I am merely the slave of the southern end of the combe. The wind blows the trees on a gray day, and it is like Aladdin rubbing his lamp; this genius is obliged to attend."

"I will have Bobbin put in the cart at once, and we will sally forth. I should love to see the 'genius' (the compliment is your own, not mine) at the beck of half a dozen Aladdins at once. How very awkward it would be to be obliged to trudge with your paint-box in three or four different directions at the same time; if you have no volition in the matter, that, of course, is quite a possible contingency."

Bobbin was a smart pony, and off they started in the sunny spring weather.

Up the nearer hills in the sunshine they drove, with the sound of the little rushing river rising to them from among the lush green meadows; into a shallower combe to the eastward, where sunken lanes were arched with branches overhead, so that, leafless as were the bushes, the sun hardly entered; stopping now beside an old pink-washed farmhouse, whose thatch was green with moss and whose gables were embowered with wildbrier that was already coming into leaf; or pausing to look over the hill to where the sunlit ridges and valleys of the moor lay steeped in a golden haze, or racing down a moorland road at a great pace till they reached a rugged valley of grassy

rocks and a ruined chapel therein — all this
they did in the first hour, but Harvey was
not yet enslaved a second time.

"Seriously, don't you think that you
ought to exercise some judgment in the matter? You will, of course, catch your death
of cold painting in the most bleak and sun-
less place in the country. It is a matter of
no importance to any one but yourself, of
course, still " —

Harvey was enjoying himself immensely,
but he was not interested in the choice of
a new subject.

"It would make a little difference to you,
would n't it? " — with that tone in his voice
which makes the most inane words important under such circumstances.

"I don't see that it would. You will
allow that if you had perished four days
ago I could not possibly have cared; and
four days does not make much difference."

"How many days will make much difference?"

"Forty, perhaps."

"Then if four, as you grant, makes some increase in your value of me, and forty will make much, each day must add something."

He was very pleased with his own arithmetic. He looked up at her as she sat on the driving - box beside him, yet expected only a humorous retort; he was conscious of a little surprise when she replied eagerly: —

"Yes, and it will take you a good many days to finish the picture, won't it? Our March winds are very bad; you see, by the time you catch consumption or pneumonia, or whatever it is, I might care a great deal. Please give up working at that picture. Mr. Knighton says that he is sure it is bad for you, coming from the south, and he is not a molly-coddle."

"Ask me something else, anything else in the world? I might as well not live as not live to the purpose for which I am made."

She touched Bobbin with the whip, and

went by the hamlet on the moor at which
the coach stopped to get a parcel, and made
the circuit back to Norcombe by the road
that lay, like the combe, in the shadow of
the hill. As they proceeded they came, not
near, but within sight of the top of the
combe.

"I wish you would not paint in that
bleak place," repeated Alice, looking towards it.

Her look reminded Harvey how she had
looked when she went past him on Sunday,
and for the first time it occurred to him to
wonder if she had a hidden reason for her
desire. It was an unpleasant suspicion,
and he felt it to be base. He only replied : —

"I saw you in the combe on Sunday."

"Yes; why did n't you speak to me when
I passed you? Did you think I was a ghost
again?"

He felt that there was not much light-
heartedness in her inquiry, but the sun,
which only shone here for a short time in

the morning, had long left, and he, sensitive
to such things, felt it to be a depressing
place.   Here there was no building within
sight except the few detached tumble-down
cottages in the hollow of the moor.   From
the chimney of one of these, the best, there
was smoke issuing.

"Surely," said Harvey, as this hamlet
came suddenly into view, "it is not like
Knighton to leave any dwelling in such a
miserable condition?"

"They are not dwellings.   He is allowing
them to fall to pieces."

"But people do live in them."   Harvey
was alert to discover a piece of landlord's
tyranny.

"What makes you think so?"   There
was curiosity in her tone.

"Naturally because I see the smoke."

"Oh, that is only old Gor's chimney.
Has not Mr. Knighton told you about old
Gor?   Gor is really her christened name;
it is in the church register.   She is more
than seventy years old, and the people think

she is a witch.  She chooses to live there.
Mr. Knighton has turned her out and put
her in a decent lodging half a dozen times;
but she always goes back, so he has given
up chevying her."

"Knighton was beaten, was he?"  Harvey chuckled at the idea of the strange con-
test.

All that week the sky was gracious and
the sun bright; Harvey could not work.
He fell into the comfortable habit of going
in and out of Norcombe House at all hours
of the day; he became personally acquainted
with Bobbin and the pigs, and learned to
distinguish one glass frame from another
and know what was inside.  This he felt to
be a triumph, for he had not much natural
aptitude for such nice distinctions.  He frequented the sitting-room, and fell into the
most brotherly ways with both the ladies.
It was a very quiet life that they all led —
a life that, as it were, opened all its doors
and windows to the village street, for the
house and park were not only in full view

of the street, but nothing went on within either that was not a matter of perfect knowledge to all the dwellers thereon.

An ill-tempered maid called Mary waited upon the two ladies and glared fiercely at Harvey whenever she had the opportunity to do so. Harvey, after making a few futile efforts to propitiate her, was sensitive enough to take a nervous dislike to her hostility. Alice laughed, but Amy Ross comforted him very kindly by explaining that she had always had precisely the same dread, but had never dared to confess it until he did. Now she was no longer ashamed; now she could frankly confess that she had always been afraid of Mary. She had been too much afraid of Alice to say this before. Alice considered that sensitiveness was synonymous with selfishness. She looked up with pretty grief toward Alice as she spoke.

"I am not conscious of ever having made such a remark," said Alice.

"Ah, but I can see it in your face, Alice;

I know by your manner that that is what you think."

The opinion that Alice was severe toward poor Amy Ross grew upon Harvey involuntarily. He began to think of her as "poor Amy;" and yet there were occasions on which she was blither than Alice: if he prepared any little surprise for them she took more delight in it than Alice did.

"I can understand her so much better than Alice can," he said to himself often, and after a while he said it to Alice, too. "You know you mean to be awfully kind, but you are not the least fitted by nature to understand Mrs. Ross."

Alice turned round to look at him, her gray eyes wide with surprise; but in a moment there was a look of amusement. "Do you *really* think you know Amy better than I, who have known her well for years?" She asked this with obvious curiosity.

"It is a matter of sympathetic temperament, not of length of time."

"It is a matter of ordinary insight and common sense; but it is just possible " — with piquant directness — "that in this matter you are not exercising either, or perhaps have not got them to exercise."

It was the first time that Alice had said anything uncomplimentary to him. He felt now that he had always known that she could be unkind by Amy's timid manner, but actually to experience it was worse.

Alice talked on. "If you saw a person in tolerable health wishing to sit by the fire all day, would you think it kinder to set him to lead an active life, or to keep heaping on the coals and arranging a draught-screen behind him? Amy is a charming woman, but she is always courting attention, *just* as children do. She is young yet, and there is lots of good in her. She can get over it; but if she does n't, it will weaken both her mind and morals. It is just like drinking, or taking opium, you know."

Harvey did not agree with this view of

Amy's character. He remembered how pretty were her eyes, and did not attempt to give any real thought to a theory which appeared to him unkind. "Two women in one house," he repeated to himself. But upon further consideration, he perfectly excused Alice. "Women," he thought, "are *never* just to one another, and it was natural enough for her to turn upon me when I took her friend's part."

## CHAPTER VII

SOME fourteen days of the forty set by Alice as a sufficient time to fall in love had elapsed. Harvey had found them amply sufficient for his own requirements. He felt himself to be deeply in love. The days had flown on wings because, although he had done some hunting, and on gray days worked at his picture, he had spent the better part of every day with the ladies of Norcombe House. On this day he had walked over to meet the coach, expecting a packet of artist's materials which had already been belated on the road. The coach was late. To his surprise, Alice came also to its stopping place in her little cart. She asked for a package of household stuff which was not there, but she did not consider that it was worth her while to wait for the coach, as her package could be fetched another day just as well.

"You are going home as soon as the coach comes in, I suppose?" she said to Harvey.

The day afterwards he remembered that she had taken the trouble to make this inquiry. She drove away, not by either road which led to Norcombe, but by a third, to a village which lay a couple of miles over the moor in the opposite direction.

The coach was very late; anything less than anxiety for his colors would not have kept Harvey so long. When at length he did set out, a heavy rain with driving wind had come on, which still longer retarded his return.

The path was a narrow lane of water. Wet, cold, and in haste, Harvey was walking, thinking of nothing, seeing nothing, but the sheets of rain, when he was suddenly forced to see Alice's cart standing among the gorse not far from the ruined cottages; a little way off he saw Alice, and with her he certainly thought that a man stood talking. He did not feel surprised, he did not realize at first that there was

need for surprise; he was sorry that she
had remained out until the storm came on,
but quickened his pace, hoping to get a lift.
A minute more, however, long before he
came near them, Alice had made her way
back to the cart and driven on. The man
seemed to have vanished; but then Harvey
reflected that he had probably had time to
move away in the intervals of his glances.

After that, as he walked on past the cottages, it occurred to him as very singular
that Alice should have taken such a length
of time to pass over the four miles she had
had to drive, and, above all, that she should
take the trouble to stop in such weather to
speak to any of the country people. It was
almost quite dark, too, altogether too late
to be out for pleasure.

He was impatient until he could ask Alice
if she had suffered from the exposure and
what had detained her, and invited himself
to breakfast with her the next day the more
speedily to satisfy himself.

Mrs. Ross was alone in the breakfast
room at first.

"Did Alice get shockingly wet?" he cried. "Is she anything the worse? Do you know what detained her last night?"

"Alice out late and wet! Oh, but she never told me! Dear Alice never confides in me! Oh, yes, Mr. Harvey; I remember now that I thought her looking very tired. You say she was wet. I remember now I felt very anxious about her; she seemed sad. Perhaps she did not change all her damp clothes." From tiredness to depression of spirits, from depression to the fear of a heavy cold, Amy's sympathetic description was traveling fast, when Alice entered the room in her ordinary bloom and equable temper.

"Alice" (this was Harvey's greeting), "who were you talking to near the moor cottages yesterday evening? Have you caught cold? What kept you out such an enormous time? I hope you did not get very wet."

It is much pleasanter, when one speaks with a little interest and excitement, to have

this morning; it is all covered with long
brown hair, with such a funny little brush
of a mane. Oh, you have no idea how
sweet it is! It stood in the grass, that
grew about as high as its knees, and it
looked just as if it quite approved of the
universe. Fancy a baby donkey patroniz-
ing the universe!"

After breakfast she wanted Harvey to go
and offer incense at the shrine of her latest
rural divinity, but he was in a bad humor
and excused himself. Then when she had
left him he grumbled a little, as was natural
enough, to Amy.

"Dear Alice!" said Amy, "but she just
likes to plague you a little. Every woman
feels that way, you know, when she begins to
realize that a man is wholly in her power."

"I am not wholly in her power," thought
Harvey to himself as he walked to the window. Still his ill humor began to abate in
the sunshine of Amy's sympathetic explanation. If Alice was only coquetting with
him, that was not quite so bad.

"I don't think she is that sort of girl."
This he said aloud, dubiously.

"Ah but"—a pause; "but I will not
tell you. You would not understand; you
would just think that I was romantic."

"*I* always understand what you say, and
I respect people most who are romantic."

Amy experienced a sensation of great
delight. "Well, you know, love is always
the same, and when a woman begins to fall
in love I do not think she is ever very different from other women, although in other
things she may be so much stronger and
wiser."

Heretofore Harvey had accepted Amy's
explanation of all Alice's odd ways as being
solely the result of his own attraction with
a grain of salt, but all the same it was a
very delightful theory to dally with, and
when Amy harped upon it her society was
very pleasing to him. He gave expression
to his doubts now, partly to provoke further
assurances from her, but partly because
logic, which in a careless mind is apt to

work slowly, was beginning to point defi-
nitely at a more serious aspect of last night's
incident.

"I don't see why falling in love, as you
say, should make Alice stay out till after
dark in a driving storm, or get out of the
cart and walk away into the heather to
speak to any one.   Why couldn't she have
called the fellow to the road?"

"Ah, you do not understand the unrest—
You see, this new love appears to her like
a traitor in her own heart.   She knows it,
and yet will not admit that she knows it.
It is anything for distraction."

Just at this moment a further thought
struck Amy, which appeared to her irresis-
tibly beautiful.   In one sense she was as
transparent as day.   Harvey perceived as
soon as she did herself that she was arrested
by a new and pleasant idea.   She had been
stitching away busily at a little schoolboy's
jacket, but now her diligence was arrested.

"Don't you think it may have been old
Gor that dear Alice was speaking to?"

Harvey threw himself into a lounging-chair near her. The question was quite uninteresting to him in itself, but the tone and the look implied a discovery.

"I don't know, I am sure, who it was. I was an eighth of a mile away, and the rain falling like sheets of glass sideways, crossways, every way. Why should she go to talk to the old crone?"

"It could not have been a man," argued Amy; "as you say, she would have called him to come to her, and, besides, Gor is very masculine-looking."

"She may be bearded as the witches in ' Macbeth ' for all I care."

Amy took up her stitching again; her little son was in his first year at school, so that the garment was not very large, but it looked heavy, coarse work for her pretty fingers.

"What of old Gor?" Harvey repeated.

"I would not tell you what I thought of, for the world, and I dare say Alice only went to speak to her out of kindness, or to give her something, Alice is so very kind and charitable."

"But tell me what you thought of?" — coaxingly.

"Oh no, I could not; it would be treason."

"Poor Alice! a traitor in her own heart and a traitor in her household! But then, if both these are loyal to me, and she has elected me to be lord of her heart, where does the treason come in?"

The logic impressed Amy, whose whole mind was given at the moment to the little problem. "Do you think I ought to tell you? Of course, you know, it is only an idea; there may be nothing in it."

"What harm can there possibly be in giving me an idea that has nothing in it?"

"But will you promise not to think Alice silly?"

"I could not possibly think that."

"That is wise of you, Mr. Harvey" (earnestly); "it is good and wise of you to think that way. Some men always think women

silly, but it is because they do not understand. A woman has reasons that a man
cannot understand, because her heart is so
deep, so tender. Ah, a woman often re-
quires to do things that seem absurd just to
stanch the bleeding of her heart, else she
would die."

Harvey had not intended to assert that
he could not think a woman silly, his remark
had applied only to Alice. He was not at
all sure at that moment that he did not
think Amy silly; but then he was not sure
that he did. Her commendation was pleasing to him, she was pleasing, and her little
mystery entertaining.

"You see," continued Amy, "just at this
time Alice must feel that the fate of her life
is trembling in the balance. Oh, if I were
in her place I would go anywhere, do anything, just to have the future lifted a little
way " —

"Most of us would do that under any
circumstances, but how is it to be managed?"

"Every one thinks that old Gor has wonderful powers of telling how an undertaking will turn out. She keeps an old pack of cards, you know, and the people consult her about everything — at least, when they can do so without Mr. Knighton knowing — it makes him frightfully angry."

"I don't believe Alice believes such rubbish."

Amy drew back a little at the quick contradiction. "Perhaps not exactly *believes*, and yet — but what harm would there be just to ask, even if she did n't believe much? But Alice, dear child, has been born and brought up here, and early training goes for so much more than what people call ' education; ' you must remember that, Mr. Harvey."

For an hour the artist soul of him was caught with a picture — Alice, the cool-headed, calm-hearted, wise Alice, driven by a new and strange passion within her heart to consult the old spae-wife, choosing the dusk of a stormy day, when the lonely

place would be more than ever lonely, standing in the driving rain, knee-deep in the
heather, till the cards were shifted and the
oracle pronounced. And what was the question thus so anxiously asked — if he, Hal
Harvey, would prove tender and true? His
heart went out in tenderness to the girl
at the mere thought of such a possibility.
Yes, it was silly, no doubt, if she did it;
but who wants a woman to be wiser?

The weak fascination of half-credence
which was supposed to have drawn Alice to
the fortune-teller, was precisely that which
reigned in Harvey's mind concerning this
explanation.

"I hope it was the old woman she was
talking to, although she may not have had
her fortune told; for, seriously, I was just
beginning to think it did not look very nice,
the way she asked me if I was going home
at once, and then drove off in the other
direction as if she was not coming down
near the combe at all, and waiting so long.
I don't mean, of course" — He stopped

hastily, recollecting that he was saying more than he had had any intention of telling of the suspicions that had begun to crowd into his mind.

But his mind would go on working in the course it had begun. The twice that he had seen her emerge, obviously agitated, from a lonely walk in the combe claimed his attention. And then she had not wanted him to paint there! He said no more to Amy, but he felt that he had good reason for wishing that he might take refuge in the theory of old Gor and the fortune-telling. And after all, why not? Amy must know Alice well. Amy, he thought, was a woman who would have quick instincts concerning any one she loved.

"You can never trust a woman when she professes to reason and theorize," he said to himself; "but her instincts are pretty sure to be correct."

## CHAPTER VIII

AMY ROSS was walking down the village to see an old woman. She was dressed in the simplest of black gowns and straw hats. Her pretty face looked bright and sweet, her light hair reflected the sunshine; she was in a happy humor, and walked with elastic step, although she was carrying a heavy basket with obvious effort. The burden was quite too heavy for her; most women would not have carried it when there was no need. A workingman, walking in the same direction, soon asked if he might be allowed to carry it for her, and the lady's thanks were so earnest and unassuming that they walked on together as very good friends. When the basket was brought to its destination, both the gift and the fair donor entered the old woman's cottage with a flood of sunshine.

Amy had a keen sense of what she would like if she was a poor old woman. She had no other standard in her charity. When among the poor she put forth all her powers of pleasing, just as she did when among richer friends; moderation in charity was a thing which from the bottom of her heart she despised. This manner of being bountiful, if it has other advantages, has certainly this one, that it elicits much expression of gratitude. In this case the look of deep and quiet happiness that came over the sensible face of the aged cottager more than satisfied the young almoner, who could well read the meaning of such indications. Amy went out again into the mild February air, her passion for approbation satisfied.

It was that perfect hour of spring, when the elms stretch out their grouping of pink buds against the sky; and the rooks in their branches begin to disturb themselves about their housekeeping; and the children come trooping from distant lanes to the schoolhouse with hazel catkins and short-stalked

primroses held tight in their little fists.
On this particular day, as Amy walked,
Harvey came up with her.

"Is it not lovely, lovely weather, Mr.
Harvey? It seems to me this morning that
it is such a beautiful world, that the whole
universe is so full of beneficence. Oh, Mr.
Harvey, did you ever read a book — I can't
exactly remember the name of it, but it was
bound in white and gold paper, a little like
a tract — not quite, you know, for the title
was up in one corner, and in tracts it is
always printed just in the middle? I can't
remember the name of the man that wrote
it, but it was all about love, you know —
charitable love, of course, about it being
the only real thing in the world. It was so
beautiful, and made one feel so good, just
as one feels on a morning like this when " —
She stopped. She could not very well
vaunt the charitable action she had just
performed.

"I am not feeling particularly blissful
this morning. To tell the truth, I am in

trouble, and I don't know exactly what to
do."

"I am so sorry. I ought to have seen
your trouble in your face, but I was absorbed in my own happiness. You see how
selfish I am!"

"I don't know that I ought to tell you
what is the matter. I frankly confess I
don't know what I ought to do."

"Do not tell me if you think you ought
not" (soothingly). "I dare say I could give
you no advice, for I am not clever. For
myself, when I am in trouble I have only a
strong *feeling* what is the course I ought to
take, and then, when I do that, it nearly
always turns out to have been the right
thing."

"Does it?" said Harvey. "I suppose
you women have a sort of instinctive wisdom that we poor duffers have to do without; that is" (he qualified his statement),
"when your hearts are right."

"Yes" (gently), "that is everything,
is n't it, to have the heart in the right place?

I don't think any one ever goes very far
wrong with a good heart; and so I think,
if you will allow me to say it, Mr. Harvey,
that *you* will not make much of a mistake,
however perplexing it may be; but I know
perplexities are very trying, I have had so
many in my own life.    But — as one grows
older one learns so many things by experience.    I am sorry you don't think you
ought to tell me, because there is one thing
that I have learned, and that is, that the
mere telling of a trouble always does one
so much good.    Do you know, positively,
before my little boy was old enough to understand, I used to tell him things that
worried and fretted me because I had no
one else to tell them to."    She had been
speaking in a low tone, and it died away
now with plaintive vibration.

Harvey was not too engrossed with himself to feel the pathos of the situation described.

"I half think I will tell you what is worrying me," he said.    "I am sure you would

advise me better than I can advise myself. Yet " —

"Don't, if you would rather not; but of course if it would be a relief to you, you may always depend upon my respecting your confidence. My husband used to say that he always felt at least *that* comfort in talking to me, because I could keep a secret."

"I don't know that if I told you it would be exactly a secret; it's just — well, I have no doubt you will have to know it before very long anyway; things can't go on as they are. It's just that I can't understand Alice."

"Ah yes, I know," — sympathetically; "lovers' quarrels are very bitter; but then " — with a sad little smile — "they don't last long, you know, Mr. Harvey."

Her last assurance did not bring that lightening of the cloud upon his face which her assurances of Alice's affection for him usually did. "I don't know, I am sure." He gave this clause of moody reserve in answer to her smile.

This difference in the tone of his mind

acted upon hers like wind on the sails of a
rudderless boat.

"I don't quite understand Alice myself."
There was just the slightest possible suggestion in her tone that there was fault somewhere.

"Mrs. Ross" (eagerly and yet with hesitation), "do you know — but of course you
must know — if Alice could possibly have
any relative or friend — a man, I mean,
hanging about here?"

Amy looked at him in surprise. "Oh
no, Alice has no relative that could possibly
be here. There is no one anywhere near
that we do not all know."

Harvey walked some paces in silence, and
then: "Well, I don't know what to make
of it" — a longer silence, gloomy and dis-
contented. "I certainly saw Alice giving
something to a fellow; he was certainly not
one of the villagers — he wore an ulster with
capes. I was a long way off, but I am sure
it was a gentleman's get-up; I am sure that
coat had been built in town."

"But where? When?" Amy cried, a little wildly.

"In the combe, not anywhere near the path, but farther up the bank among the trees. It was at eight o'clock this morning; of course, she did not expect me or any one else to be within sight so early."

"It couldn't have been Alice! But she did start at seven to go in that direction, and take breakfast with Mr. Knighton, and go over all her accounts with him. She always goes to him after every quarter-day, and he helps her to — what is it you call it? — audit, you know. He breakfasts at eight, and she went on foot, so, of course, she might have been in the combe; but I am sure she wouldn't go to speak to a man. It could not have been Alice you saw, Mr. Harvey."

"I beg your pardon. I have no wish to contradict you."

"I ought not to have contradicted you" — meekly.

"There is such a lot of holly there, I

don't know where the fellow went to — I don't care either, not a particle; but I hallooed to Alice, so she stopped until I could get down to her " —

He stopped here, not as if he had at first intended to, but as suddenly remembering cause for reserve.

There was a degree of shocked excitement in Amy's mind which blunted her perception of his reticence. "You spoke to her; and what did she say? Who was the other gentleman? "

"'Say,' why she said, ' Good-morning,' and that it was a fine day, and that she had not expected me to be out so early, and would I come with her and breakfast with Mr. Knighton, — she was sure he would be very glad."

"But you asked whom she had been speaking to? " (most earnestly).

"She said that she was in a great hurry, that she was late for her engagement with Mr. Knighton, and he was so particular that he would be angry."

"But you did not let her go, or you went with her? You insisted upon knowing something about this stranger, that at least he was a proper acquaintance for her?"

"Oh, I let her go to take breakfast with Knighton. Why should I not?" (with offended dignity). "It may be all one to me very soon whom she takes breakfast with. I saw her safe on to the highroad and let her go."

"Oh, but Mr. Harvey "—

Amy turned upon Harvey a face that was positively pale with dismay, and he, though he had been excessively piqued before, had not felt the full force of the suspicions to which Alice's conduct gave rise until now.

"Of course," he said, "she had to make some answer when I asked her who the fellow was; she said she would speak to me again about it when she came back to luncheon."

"Oh!" (eagerly); "then she will tell you — then she will explain everything."

"I am not at all sure that she means to

be frank. I think she was only putting me
off to gain time."

Harvey continued walking in silence at
Amy's side with a mind highly perturbed.

An old woman came suddenly hobbling
out of the gardener's cottage in the park,
and stopped when she found herself directly
in their path.

"Good-morning, Gor," said Amy; "how
is your rheumatism to-day?"

The witch dropped a bob curtsey, but she
eyed them both sharply. The sunbonnet
she wore shaded, but did not conceal, the
brown face that was handsome despite its
withered skin.

The carpet was of grass and daffodil
clumps, the roof of lofty elm branches, that
held small pink blossoms scattered under
the sky; behind the crone was a white cottage on which white jasmine climbed to a
faded thatch. The three human figures tarried there while Amy did her duty in speaking to the old woman, her manner patient
as one who could set aside her own trouble
when needful for the good of another.

"Is there anything I can do for you, Gor — were you wanting anything?" The mixture of awe and condescension in Amy's manner made Harvey bend an interested glance upon the witch.

"Well, I coomed vor a sup o' soup Miss told I to fetch, but I be main glad to zet eyes zo close on young meäster that folks bees a-talken aboot. The day afore he cwome I saw un in a bucket o' water I fetched vrom the stream."

"Oh, Gor, you know you ought not to talk in that way. Mr. Knighton does not allow it."

"Oh, as to Zquire, her did zay a sdrange thing that very day; her zaid that even a small thing like a beätle as crawls must allus be a-usen a bit moor sense nor he have or he'd soon be having no feälers an' his children less nor none, and much moor a man wi' legs an' eyes — ay, an' Zquire be moor nor common wise."

"A little off it," said Harvey in an undertone to Amy; and then he sighed, for his trouble of mind rushed back afresh after the minute's respite.

"I did zee young meäster afore he cwome," reasserted the witch, "an' I did knaw of a thing as would make un need to zee moor of the world than her can touch an' moor of a leädy than her face. But there be eyes that can zee a face an' eyes that can zee behind that; and there be zoom times when looken sharp 's needed moor nor other times."

"What do you mean?" asked Harvey roughly.

Then he walked on. He assumed that the hag had some knowledge of Alice's secret and wanted to trade upon it. He was too much offended to listen, but no thought entered his mind that he had received any warning concerning the fair woman at his side. With a curious suggestion of mockery in her parting curtsey the old woman hobbled away.

"Oh, why did you not stop and question her?" asked Amy.

"She has seen Alice with that fellow, and knows as much as I do about it, and no more."

Then Amy and Harvey moved on, a very picture of graceful youth well met, well mated, passing through the sylvan scene.

"I can't tell you, Mr. Harvey," — Amy's low voice broke a long silence which had already said more than her words now did, — "how troubled and afraid I feel. I don't know what I am afraid of; like you, I don't know what to think. Perhaps, when I have had time, I shall see what it all means better, but — oh, how I wish I knew that dear Alice had not got into any trouble! I — I don't know whether I ought to say it — I have feared for a long time" — (The low words came hurriedly tripping after one another and as hurriedly stopped.)

Harvey's heart almost stood still with a stern fear.

"Yes, tell me," he demanded in a hard cold voice; "it is right that I should know."

"It is only that I have felt — that if dear

Alice would not embrace the truth of religion — it is hard, you know, to speak about
the things that one has felt most deeply and
prayed " — ( here her voice failed).   " But
on any one, even on any of us, without religion there is no dependence to be placed —
one does not know where one might end."

Harvey walked up to the house-door very
gloomily.  He did not realize that what
Amy had last said had not exactly fulfilled
the fear that had come to him of what she
was going to say, because he was absorbed
in thinking how true it was that a woman
without religion might fall into temptations
that would not otherwise assail her.

## CHAPTER IX

MR. KNIGHTON's great library wore an
unusual appearance of comfort and good
cheer on the morning when Alice Bolitho
came to breakfast, and then sat at his study
table for a couple of hours, learning to be
her own steward. The master of the house
always was at some pains (but this Alice
did not know) to put the room in good order
for her; he put all his papers in piles,
square and tidy, jerked the string of each
window-blind so that that article, as if in
hasty fear, suddenly rolled itself up all out
of sight and left the three small Gothic windows with their strong oak mullions entirely
bare to the morning sunlight, and then (no
one knew it but the servants) he would go
out and, to the gardener's dismay, break
off the stems of whatever choice flowers
were to be found and place them himself in

an old silver tankard for which Alice had a liking. And Alice coming in from the breakfast-parlor, had only a vague notion that the tables were always neat and the room always flooded with sunshine, and the tankard always blossoming over.

This morning Alice was glad to be rid of the presence of the fat footman who, like a robin in scarlet vest, hopped round the breakfast-table; she was even glad to bid good-day to a certain good old aunt who dwelt with Knighton, and to come into the library alone with him. It was just the sense of rest and quiet that relieved her, for she had no intention of talking secrets. She sat down to her work, but she was not intelligent over it. We all know that when the attention wanders just when the addition of a column of figures is not quite finished, the most thorough knowledge of mathematics, even in the higher branches, will not avail to bring the sum to a speedy conclusion. Then when Mr. Knighton was going through the pros and cons with regard to

an alteration in a certain lease, Alice was
found to be drawing a landscape of the
combe on the margin of her account-book,
and when questioned was obliged, shocked
with herself, to confess that she had not listened to a single word. Knighton's time
was too valuable to be tampered with in
this way.

"I deserve it, so I hope you are angry.
It would be simple and natural if you
looked enraged, and then I should be frightened into attending."

In the bottom of his heart he wished that
he could attain to this degree of nature and
simplicity, but he could not.

"You are so patient with me, Mr. Knighton, ever since I began this horrid course
of duplicity and evil-doing. You used to
scold; I wish you would scold again; I am
not so far gone but what I can be reclaimed
if you scold properly."

His patience with her, if it dated from
the time to which she alluded, dated also
from the time of Harvey's arrival, when a

certain hope within his own heart, never very strong, had at last expired, but he did not explain that to her.

"Since you have mentioned it, how is this course of evil deeds progressing?"

She sat making little marks with her pen.

"I beg your pardon," he said again. "I did not mean to ask you to say more than just what you might be willing to say in general terms."

"I wish I might tell you. Sometimes, very often, it makes me dreadfully unhappy, but then my health is so good, you see, that usually I feel that as I am not responsible in any way, it does not matter to me."

"But"— in urgent expostulation.

"Yes, I know it sounds ridiculous and silly, and impossible; still I have read of like circumstances happening in a book. There is nothing new in the horrid things people do."

"Is the matter not serious after all, that you speak of it in this way? When we last talked "—

"Oh yes," she interrupted, "in one aspect of the case it is serious, of terrible importance to somebody else, but as far as it is connected with me it is just ridiculous" — a pause. "I am afraid I have not made things any plainer."

Her arm was lying loosely on a big pile of leather-bound books, and she laid her forehead on her arm now and gave a little nervous laugh.

In a minute he said abruptly, "As I was saying, the lease as it stands was drawn up five years ago, and " — He went on with a tedious repetition of all that he had said before, and this time Alice listened. "I have now," he concluded, "put before you all the arguments that I know of in the interest of the tenant, and all those to be considered in your own interest as opposed to his; it is for you to decide between them."

"Which would you do in my place, Mr. Knighton?"

"That is not the question."

She pulled herself up wearily to consider her judgment; and when it was given they went on to other things. But during the whole morning one thought more than any of the business in hand ran in her mind; at last it found words again.

"Hal Harvey has found out that I am up to some mischief."

"He can hardly have found out that."

"That is what he thinks he has discovered."

"What has he seen?"

"I am afraid he will be sure to tell you, so I may as well. He saw me speaking to a stranger that I met in the combe this morning before I came here."

"Why did you not ask Harvey to keep your secret from me, rather than tell me that there is a man in the place into whose business I am not to inquire?"

"I thought he had taken the huff; he looked like it."

"You are hard on him, when he sees you in communication with a fellow, to give him no explanation."

"Yes, but he must know, of course, that I would not do anything he need fret about. Why, he wants me to marry him!"

## CHAPTER X

Amy Ross and Hal Harvey had sat a
full hour together in the Norcombe sitting-
room when Alice was descried entering the
gates. Amy was quite trembling with excitement. She felt that Harvey was very
angry; she could not think that he had not
just cause. At the sight of Alice she betook herself at once to her own room. She
locked herself in in her agitation, and then
began to weep. She said to herself most
fervently that she hoped there was no quar-
rel going on downstairs, that she hoped
Alice had not — Here her imagination
failed, for she had not yet decided whether
the mysterious stranger was a clandestine
lover, or whether he was a levier of black-
mail, — the two explanations which had occurred to her as most probable during the
time which had intervened between the pres-

ent minute and that in which she had said truly that she did not know what to fear. Amy paced her room and listened in an agony of impatience for sounds in the house that would proclaim that the interview was at an end.

Alice had come up the drive, and Harvey was waiting for her at the house-door. She looked tired, but she was cheerful. She smiled to him as she came up, but became grave at his imperturbable gravity.

"Have you been long here?" she asked. "Are you going to stay for dinner?"

Alice Bolitho took dinner at one o'clock and did not call it lunch.

"I don't know; you said you would speak to me now, and so I am here."

"Well"—a little wearily; "come into the sitting-room."

So they went in, and he shut the door. Alice turned round and faced him, drawing off her gloves.

"Don't look so grave, Hal. There is really nothing for you to be troubled about."

She paused a moment, and then, more slowly: "I have done nothing wrong. It surely does not need that I should assure you of that in words, but still I am willing to make the assertion if that will help you. I am very sorry indeed that I could not tell you who it was you saw me speak to this morning; I am still more sorry that I cannot tell you now, because I see that you are worrying about it; but I will tell you that the *only* reason that I do not tell is that I made a very solemn promise that I would not, and I can say, too, that my speaking to that man (she paused, choosing her words) affects me very little and does not affect you at all, except" — she blushed — "as far as you may think that everything that affects me affects you. In a few days I shall probably be able to tell you all about it; some time I shall certainly tell you."

"Alice, this mystery is intolerable."

"Do you really consider that life has become intolerable because your curiosity on a certain point must wait awhile before it

is satisfied?" She laughed at his grave
face and began mocking gently: "Dear,
dear! here is a young man with good food
and good clothes, and a congenial profession, in which he has good hope of attain-
ing wealth and eminence, and he has good
friends, too, to entertain him every day,
and yet he finds life intolerable because,
like Bluebeard's wife, there is one door
that he may not unlock!"

"It is not that, Alice; it is not mere
curiosity."

"Well, what is it, then?"

Harvey hesitated, stammered something,
and stopped. He began to realize that she
had put him in a very difficult position. If
he believed implicitly what she had just said
there could be nothing of all his apprehension and displeasure left but mere curiosity;
but then, how could what she had said possibly be true? He remembered the series
of circumstances, each small in itself, that
he had against her; he remembered very
vividly the interview he had beheld from

a distance that morning; he began now to have a sense that Alice was too clever altogether, because she had so speedily cornered him and put him at this disadvantage. How could he tell her that he did not believe her? At the very thought of that he recoiled, not only from the statement, but from its truth; it was impossible to stand there beside her and think that she was telling lies. He took refuge in a mental shuffle.

"Why did you give this solemn promise?"

"I cannot tell you that, because it would be telling too much."

"I did not like the look of the fellow I saw this morning. I only saw his back, but I have seen a good deal of the world, and there was something, I can't tell exactly what, horribly objectionable about him."

She remained quite silent; she did not even look as if the character of the man was of the slightest importance.

"How did he get into the combe this morning? and where did he disappear to?"

Instead of looking as if she were in the wrong, it appeared that she seemed to think that it was she who had need of patience.

"Is it kind of you to ask me when I have told you I cannot tell?"

"Oh! Alice" (his voice faltered), "it is not as if my happiness were not bound up in your welfare." He turned and walked to the window.

She took off her hat and jacket slowly, but held them in one hand, as if waiting until he should finish what he had to say. Harvey looked out, turned back and glanced at her, looked out once more. He was intensely uncomfortable through it all. The feeling that in her presence had been gradually growing upon him was that he must trust her, that he could not do anything else.

Harvey turned at last with the lighter heart that came with a genuine longing for reconciliation; forgetting in the strength of the moment that it was for the first time, he gently took both her hands in his own.

"Alice, I hope that it is all just as I understand from your words " —

A flash came into her eyes as she drew back and looked at him with some disdain. "Do you mean to say that you hope that what I have said is true?"

It was perhaps precisely what he had meant, but another meaning was there also, and he took refuge in that. "I have no doubt that you think what you have said," — tardy as was this credence he did actually give it at this moment, — "but you may trust others too far; you may think that it is right for you to do what is not really safe or right. How can I help being troubled and apprehensive?"

She had not actually withdrawn her passive hands from his, and now she relaxed a little her arms which she had stiffened. "It is not, perhaps, much more complimentary to think that I am easily duped, but still " — her face began to resume its usual cheerfulness, and after a moment's hesitation she finished archly — "if that is the best

that you can do I suppose I must put up
with it and bear it patiently; and now tell
me quick if you are going to stay for dinner, for I must tell Mary."

"But, Alice " —

"Dinner or no dinner? This is the third
time of asking; speak now or ever after do
without it."

It was she who forgave him, and held out
as it were her sceptre to be kissed. Harvey was left with an odd feeling of having
been forced into a mental somersault, but
still in some way he seemed to have come
up head first and smiling. After all, the
form of the reconciliation was a mere trifle;
if only his mind had been really at rest
about Alice he would not have given another thought to her arrogant little ways.

The first sound that Amy heard in her
chamber overhead was the prosaic dinner-
bell. She was disappointed, but she thought
she was relieved and glad.

## CHAPTER XI

THAT evening it was Harvey who sought Knighton's company. After some search and inquiry, the servants informed the caller that the master was inspecting some cattle in one of the meadows. Harvey, declining to wait, went thither accordingly. It was about six o'clock on a gusty evening; the air and the ground were dry; the sun had just gone down.

"I am quite at leisure," Mr. Knighton said, when he heard that the young man wished to have some particular talk with him.

So they walked slowly across the low-lying fields, known in the neighborhood as "the marshes."

Knighton gave Harvey his whole attention, but he did not give him the least help in striking into the heart of his subject. Harvey found it much more difficult than he expected to tell what he had to tell, although he certainly experienced no interruption. The young steers, clustered here and there near their path, were not more dumb and patient than the listener.

At last it was Knighton's turn to speak. "I understand, then, that you consider that Miss Bolitho is in some way in jeopardy, because you have seen her once at dusk speaking to some one who might have been the old fortune-teller, and once speaking to an unknown gentleman. What sort of danger is it, may I ask, that you apprehend?"

"You see, I can't quite avoid taking this into consideration: if I had not unluckily or luckily, as the case may be, settled on that particular spot to live and work in, I should have seen nothing of all this. It's only by the merest accident that Alice was compelled to place in me the scant confidence of telling me there was something she will not tell."

"To confide may be a virtue or a vice; it depends entirely upon circumstances."

The retort rose to Harvey's lips that he

would be very sorry to have a wife who
should ever consider confidence in him a
vice, but the statement, like many that one
makes in ill temper even to one's self, he
knew covered more ground than he could
seriously adhere to, and Knighton's presence did not encourage rashness. He contented himself with saying, —

"You cannot expect me to rest in a secure
feeling that she is in no danger?"

"No, I can hardly expect that."

"Then what am I to do?"

"You admit that it is merely by an accident that you have discovered these inci-
dents, and against Miss Bolitho's desire. If
that accident had not occurred you would of
course be under no responsibility to act.
Does the accidental acquirement of knowledge, that you were not meant or desired
to have, alter the case?"

"It must materially alter my peace of
mind."

"I should be disposed to grant that,
whether you will or no, your mind is proba-

bly not entirely under your control; but your actions are, and the point, as I take it, for you to decide is, whether you are justified in taking action."

"You surely do not think that I ought to behave as if I did not know, when I do know?"

"That is a matter entirely for your own decision. I merely wished to point out where in that direction your decision lay."

"Do you think" — indignantly — "that it is right for a young girl in Alice's position to be behaving this way?"

"It does not appear to me right, but I do not know in the least what motives actuate her, or what circumstances have given rise to those motives."

"Well, it seems to me that it is time we did know."

They walked on for some distance. Dusk was falling upon the high moors, upon sloping pastures and groves and the long meadows that lay on either side of the little river.

"I am determined to do something," said

Harvey. "If I could be content myself,
Mrs. Ross is very much alarmed, and women, of course, must be pretty safe guides
where a woman's safety is concerned."

"Did Miss Bolitho take Mrs. Ross into
her confidence?"

"No; if she had the whole thing would
look much fairer. But Alice is young, and
I don't know, but I fancy, the reason of her
being so unresponsive to Mrs. Ross's affection is that Mrs. Ross is not inexperienced
enough to be a companion exactly on her
own level, that is, she would naturally attempt some gentle restraint, and that, on the
other hand, she is not old enough to be entirely without some appearance, as it were,
of rivalry. Women are so apt, you know,
to look upon another woman as a rival,
although there may not be the slightest
cause for it, that is, until the experience of
trouble, and that sort of thing, gives them
broader views. Of course I don't pretend
to know exactly what the cause of Alice's
jealousy is; one might conjecture a thou-

sand things and not hit on exactly the right one; but I was sitting an hour with Mrs. Ross this morning waiting for Alice to come in, and from several things she let fall, quite unintentionally, I could see that the state of the case was pretty much as I have said. Of course Alice is a very sweet girl, a dear girl, and whenever I am with her I feel as if she were all perfection, but it stands to reason that she must just have her failings, like all other girls."

"Alice Bolitho has her faults. I should not have thought that they lay in the direction in which you indicate, but "—dryly— "you perhaps have had opportunity for more correct observation."

"Well, yes, I have been with her pretty constantly, day in and day out, for the last three weeks, and then the sort of relationship, in love with her as I am, without any particular spooniness to blind me — that of course is the way to know a girl thoroughly."

"As you say, you could hardly have had

a more perfect opportunity for study of a character. It appears to me that your present course must depend entirely on two questions: in the first place, whether you can trust Miss Bolitho to do what is right without your interference, and in the second place, whether you can trust her to do what is wise."

"Well, if it comes to that, I don't think a girl of twenty-four is a Solomon, even if she has been to Cambridge, probably the less for that, because it is common sense that is wanted here; and Mrs. Ross thinks that Alice ought to be saved from herself; she said so quite distinctly to me this afternoon when I told her that Alice had declined to confide in me; and Mrs. Ross ought to know Alice thoroughly."

"Yes, you are quite right; Mrs. Ross *ought* to know her."

Harvey was pleased with this agreement, for before this he had had a notion that Knighton had imbibed a false idea of Amy, probably from Alice's misrepresentation.

## CHAPTER XII

HARVEY'S first move, in the new game of chess that he set himself to play, was to give up all his days to visiting at Norcombe House, and with fond insistence he refused to let Alice drive or walk alone. For a few days Alice gave in to all this with the utmost good nature, but there gradually came to be a slight difference in her manner to him. He felt that he was not nearer to but farther from her at the end of a few days of this very close companionship; it was, however, only a feeling; he could point to no definite proof.

On the afternoon of the fifth day, Alice, according to a long appointment, was fetched by Mr. Knighton's carriage to meet him at an outlying farmhouse which belonged to her, to consider a question of repairs. It was a brougham which came, and a relative of Mr. Knighton's was already in it.  Harvey remained at home.

He nodded gayly to the occupants of the carriage as he stood bareheaded in a drizzling rain to see them start.  It was impossible to have been with Alice those four days and feel that any direful project was brewing.  Harvey was glad to have this opportunity to talk the matter over again with Amy; he turned into the sitting-room with alacrity.  In these days, gray and sunny alike, even his dearest picture was neglected.

Whenever Amy was left alone she had a way of suddenly bestirring herself to make the room more to her taste.  Alice had not Amy's disposition to be lavish in the matter of coals upon the fire, or butter upon the toast for tea, or the best cushions from the rarely used drawing-room thrown into the sitting-room chairs.  When Harvey took tea with Amy alone, as had more than once before to-day been the case, he enjoyed unwonted luxury, although he was too thor-

ough a man to know what went to make up
the difference.

"I wish Alice would tell me what she
had to do with that fellow the other day."
Harvey sank into an armchair.

That he should begin upon the subject
thus easily, lounging as he spoke, showed
that it had already lost much of its former
darkness in his mind.

"I am so glad, Mr. Harvey, that you can
speak of it so easily.  You can't think how
it comforts me, for it makes me feel that I
am foolish, and that after all there is not so
much to dread.  The strong calm way that
men take things is, I suppose, the really
wise way, and it is such a help to us poor
women, who are all imagination and nerves,
to rest upon it."

"I am not at all easy in my mind," replied Harvey, growing more grave.

He had had half a notion, as he sat down,
of pointing out to Amy that her delicate
nervous organization had caused her to exaggerate the matter, but as she was aware

of it, his caution was unnecessary; and fur-
thermore, but this he felt only indistinctly,
as she was aware of this tendency her judgment could not have been led far astray by
it.

"You know," Harvey began again (his
mind was arguing with itself, and so having
made a remark on one side, he now made
one on the other), "Knighton did n't really
seem much disturbed when I went and told
him all about it. Of course he admitted
that you and I, knowing Alice best, were
better able to judge than he, but I really
think he thought that I need n't take any
precautions."

"I did not know you had consulted Mr.
Knighton. If I had known you were going
to — but no, it does n't matter."

"What does n't matter? What were you
going to say?"

There was a lengthy pause, and Amy
sighed. Her pretty face was white and
wan. Her bright eyes had a pathetic look,
and her aspect truly represented her condi-

tion. In the last days she had sedulously avoided remaining an unnecessary minute in the company of the two friends; she did this under an exaggerated idea of the happiness that it gave Alice to have Harvey's undisturbed attention, and this very exaggeration made her own lot seem more bitter by contrast. She was not in love with Harvey; she did not wish to marry him; she had not thought of such a thing; but the fact that Alice had suddenly become of so much importance to some one, to a man, too (and Amy, by her very nature, regarded men as infinitely more interesting than women), made her feel rather than think herself unkindly treated. Alice, too, Amy felt certain, had not treated her with half the consideration, since Harvey came, that she had given before. She brooded over this a good deal.

As these two sat together just then, Harvey saw Amy's emotion, and knew that it was genuine. To see this, and to infer, first, that it arose from the cause to which

she assigned it, solicitude for Alice's safety,
and second, that it was well for him to con-
sole her, appeared to him all one act of
mind; like all untrained observers, he did
not distinguish that which he perceived from
that which he inferred from it:

"When I see you so concerned for Alice's
welfare I feel more than ever that she is
treating both you and me rather cavalierly,"
said he.

Now Amy had braced herself up in the
last days to acquiesce in the belief, which
was her inference from his close companionship with Alice, that he had learned entirely
to disregard her own fears, and that nothing
she could say would ever have any influence
over him again. She had decided, in a
plaintive, resigned way, that she would suffer her anxiety alone and make no further
efforts to coerce others into measures which
appeared to her desirable. Now, however,
it seemed to her that Providence must intend that, after all, she should be of some
service to these young people at this criti-

cal juncture. To be of service, with her experience of life and true womanly instincts — this was really what she thought she aimed at.

"If I had known that you were going to speak to Mr. Knighton, I think perhaps I ought to have told you — as a friend, perhaps it would have been only fair just to set you on your guard. I have often thought, although I may be quite wrong, that he is in love with Alice himself."

"You think so! no? Oh, I think you must be mistaken about that, Mrs. Ross. He is a fossil as to heart or emotion, or anything of that sort, — quite a fossil, I am sure."

"Of course I may be mistaken,"— meekly, — "but if it were so, and he heard from you that she was in any trouble, it would not be in nature that he should wish *you* to rescue her; he would rather plan to do it himself."

"Yes, of course, if he felt that way; but I think, if you will excuse my saying so, that in this you are mistaken, Mrs. Ross. Why, if your surmise is correct, did he not ask Alice to marry him long ago? But" — more complacently — "of course she may have refused him."

"Oh, no," — quickly; "I am sure she did not refuse him."

"Indeed!" — with a graver interest. "What makes you so sure?"

Amy's assurance in reality was hers most naturally by virtue of the fact that Alice was so unaccustomed to concealment that if this important thing had occurred in her life, her friend in all probability would have known it; but when Amy came to consider the cause of her assurance, other and more interesting ideas occurred to her mind.

"Oh, I don't know," — evasively; "you would hardly expect any girl in this part of the country to refuse Mr. Knighton, would you, Mr. Harvey? You would not have expected the beggar maid to have refused King Cophetua."

"I am sure Alice is not at all the sort of

girl just to take him because he is rich,"—
with offended decision.

"Oh, I did not mean to imply that,"—
eagerly; "not for a moment!"

Which assertion, being interpreted, meant
that she had no intention of implying anything that Harvey would censure or emphat-
ically disagree with, and as to Alice, she
did not know what she did mean to imply;
it was a new idea and she was only working
it out. She was unhappy, and threw off
unhappy suggestions to ease herself, with
no realization of their effect.

Harvey did not continue his questions on
this particular. It appeared to him that
there was only one remaining conclusion,
and that was, that Alice had that degree of
affection for Mr. Knighton which warranted
Amy in being certain that she would marry
him if she could.

"Knighton has had a clear field all these
years," he remarked solemnly. "If he
wants Alice, why has n't he asked her?"

"Ah, well, that is not quite so easy to

say." Amy spoke with a pretty, plaintive air of reflection. "I think it very probable he could not quite explain it himself, but you see " — Knighton might not know his own circumstances, but Amy, after a moment's thought, saw them clearly — "you see, Mr. Harvey, Mr. Knighton is what might be called a confirmed bachelor, and that class of men, you know, are always very slow to move. They think of the extra expense of keeping a wife, and of the breaking up of their habits, and loss of their freedom, and all that, so they wait, letting one month and another slip by until some one else steps in; and Mr. Knighton is far too proud, of course, to come into rivalry with you or any one else who, in his pride, he might think at all inferior."

"He has been very kind and civil to me," Harvey said doubtfully.

"Oh, yes, of course he would be that; he would consider it due to his pride and to his position."

Harvey sat thinking, and not pleasantly.

He had come a perfect stranger into this
neighborhood, and had taken for granted
that his friends in it felt as they appeared
to feel, and were related to himself and to
each other as they appeared to be.  He,
being honest, had supposed other people
were honest, but of course it was quite possible that if this assumption was false,
things might be quite otherwise than as
they had appeared to him.  Amy had made
a revelation that was astounding; he could
not have imagined, up to that moment, that
she or any one could believe Knighton and
Alice to be in love with one another; it
never occurred to him to consider that such
an ostentatiously conscientious person as
Amy might have spoken thus without wholly
believing it.  Although it might not be so
bad as she supposed, yet, as she believed
it, there must be some foundation for her
belief.  Perhaps it was true on one side, if
not on the other.  Partly because of that
tendency to self-aggrieving which most characters possess more or less, perhaps because

he thought Amy more likely to be informed in one case than in the other, he was more ready to believe Alice to be in fault than Knighton. He remembered now that she had always kept him, Harvey, at arm's length. He had considered the understanding between them as proof that he was an admitted lover, but he could not at this moment think of any positive evidence that she felt affection for him.

Amy, who had merely chanced on the subject of Knighton by accident, now began on a theme in which her thoughts had been at large for some days.

"I think I know what may be the nature of the trouble under which poor Alice is laboring; at least I *hope* that what I have thought of may be the explanation. After talking to you the other day I remembered what I thought might possibly throw light upon it. Soon after her grandfather died, Alice got a letter which she showed me. She tried to appear as if she was not much disturbed by it, but I knew at the time

that it must have distressed her very much.
One can know so well how people are thinking and feeling by the way they look, even
when they are outwardly composed — can't
one, Mr. Harvey?"

"Of course, of course" — with impatient
certainty.

"The letter was from a person — I don't
know exactly from whom; I think he lived
in Bristol; but he roundly accused Alice's
father, you know, of owing him money;
fifty pounds, I think he said, would cover
the debt and the interest.   He said he had
kept quiet during the old man's lifetime out
of respect for him.   I feel certain now, in
looking back, that the letter hinted decidedly that there was some disgrace attaching
to him about owing this money.   Yes, I feel
quite convinced that it was even more than a
hint, a pretty clear assertion that it was so."

"What did Alice say?   What did Alice
do?   I feel certain the man was an impostor, but Alice might not think of that; she
would be very much troubled."

"Yes, I am sure she was very much troubled. I felt very sorry for her at the time — oh, very sorry; but Alice never confides in me, you know," — a little pathetic smile and a shake of the head, — "oh, never in me."

"I am very sorry she does not " — sincerely.

"I feel convinced now, looking back, that she hid her real intentions from me, in which, of course, I should be the last to blame her, as her father's good name is involved; or, at least," — with hesitating deference to his opinion, — "if the man was an impostor, she thought it was involved. But when she showed me the letter she asked me if it was not funny. I did not disguise from her that I did not think it funny; I thought it was a very serious matter. So then I think that she realized, what perhaps she had not seen at first, that it was serious."

"It sounds to me like a case of arrant imposition."

"Even so, don't you think that the of-
fender ought to have been dealt with and
severely punished? That was, of course,
what I meant when I said to Alice it was
serious." (The sweet musical tone here had
just a touch of severity.)

"Yes, of course," said Harvey.

"But Alice, dear girl, no doubt, thought
that I meant that the claim was a just one,
and indeed, for aught I know, the claim
and the accusation may have been just; but
anyway, to make a long story short, Alice
did not confide in me any further; all that
she did was to put the letter in her pocket
and say that she would show it to Mr.
Knighton the next time she saw him."

"Well, that was really the most sensible
thing she could do, was n't it?"

"Yes, I quite approved of her intentions,
I assure you; but I do not believe now that
she did speak to Mr. Knighton. Perhaps "
— doubtfully — "she may have meant to
do just what she told me, and afterwards
changed her mind, or " — a little pause for

consideration — "she may have been so shocked at the idea of her father's honesty being called into question that she may have hardly known what she was saying in her efforts to make me believe that she thought nothing of it, and to put the matter out of my mind."

Harvey considered these two alternatives for a moment. "I think she probably meant to do as she said, but it is easy to change one's mind."

"I collect stamps," Amy continued. "I don't mean curious stamps, but any common kind; for a thousand of them will buy a Chinese baby."

"I beg your pardon — will buy what?"

"A dear little baby girl in China, you know, from being thrown into the water, so that the missionaries can bring her up."

"Oh, yes, I understand" (which was untrue, for he did not).

"And so I keep all the old envelopes that are thrown into the waste-paper basket, and then when I have time I cut the stamps out.

But I often let a great many collect before I cut them, and the other night when I thought of it I could not rest, but got up and looked over them; and it was just as I thought : there were two others from Bristol addressed to Alice in that person's handwriting. I am sure I remember the handwriting perfectly, and both these "— in a low, important voice — "bore postmarks of a later date than the letter which was shown to me, so of course it is clear that she never consulted Mr. Knighton. He would never have allowed her to correspond with a person of that sort. Indeed, don't think I blame her! Inexperienced, of course, at her age she must be; but, granting that, what could be a more praiseworthy feeling than the desire to keep secret a father's fault; and of course Mr. Knighton would be the last person she would wish to know it. He is so proud and censorious."

"Certainly the last person, if she is in love with him," thought Harvey.

"Then, you see, as she always shows her

books to Mr. Knighton, and as he knows
all that goes on about the bank, she could
not draw all the fifty pounds at once without arousing his suspicions. Nor could she
very well send a check to this person, because, of course, Mr. Knighton would find
out."

"I must say Knighton seems to keep a
pretty close eye on her affairs."

"Yes, he does keep a pretty close eye
upon anything connected with money matters; ' close ' " — sadly — "is just the ad-
jective I should use."

"Yet he seems liberal enough."

"*Noblesse oblige*, you know. He has
such a magnificent idea of himself. But I
beg of you, Mr. Harvey, not to run away
with the idea that I am saying anything
against Mr. Knighton. I would not for
the world. I think he is a truly good man.
We have all our faults, and of course I may
be mistaken in my estimate of his."

"Well, but do you mean to say you
think that Alice is making appointments

every now and then with this Bristol fellow,
and giving him this precious fifty pounds
by degrees?"

"Oh, Mr. Harvey, I do hope that it is
that.   Is it not much more likely that Alice
would do a thing that is, if mistaken, at least
high-minded, than that she would do anything that was wrong?   I can't help hoping
that her secret is just about this money."

Harvey did not reply for some time.
The hope that Amy expressed so eagerly
implied a fear he could not discuss.   He
sat looking into the fire.   Even if this supposition about the money were true, Harvey
could not admire Alice's course of action.
Of course, to shield a father's name a young
girl is supposed to endure all agonies cheer-
fully; but that she should deliberately hood-
wink three people who would each and all
have been as zealous to shield and defend
that name as herself, was not Harvey's
notion of high-mindedness.

Amy was quite carried on now by the
interest of her discovery.   "Oh, of course

it is only a surmise," she said, "and, you
know, I never place very much confidence
in my own surmises; but, Mr. Harvey,
there is another little fact that points in the
same way. You know dear Alice is a little
careless; young people often are. Even if
she had a secret I would not expect her to
keep it very carefully; and the other day,
the night before she took her books over to
Mr. Knighton, she asked me to check a
little sum she had been doing of the entries
in her check-book, and I could not help
noticing that for the last four weeks she
had drawn several pounds more than usual.
Now I am sure, Mr. Harvey, that it has
not been expended on the housekeeping, and
still more sure that Alice has not been buy-
ing anything expensive for herself."

Harvey suddenly rose from his chair and
went over to a small table near the window.
Alice was not a person who troubled herself
about keys; her housekeeping-book and her
private account-book, with larger books for
other business entries, always lay on this

table, and it was only a day or two since
Harvey had superintended the addition of
a week's entry in them all, read off the
items and turned over the leaves freely with
Alice's approval. It did not occur to him
until the books were in his hand that it was
a somewhat different thing to examine the
same figures in Alice's absence.

"Perhaps I had better not," he said,
shoving back the unopened books. Then
to Mrs. Ross: "But surely you have taxed
Alice with this? Wouldn't it be far the
simplest way just to tell her that you suppose she has kept it a secret for her father's
sake, but that you have guessed what it is?
She would rather know what you suspect
her of, I am sure."

"Oh, Mr. Harvey, I beg and pray — oh,
you have no idea how severe Alice can be.
She cannot endure that I should even make
a remark sometimes, much less know a thing
that she does not want me to know."

"I am sorry that Alice should seem to
you such a bear " — seriously.

"I did not mean to say that. Indeed"
— with trembling agitation — "I did not
mean to say anything against Alice."

"No, you are kindness itself, Mrs. Ross;
you would not intentionally detract from
any one, but I think you must surely misunderstand Alice."

"You know, I dare say, I have annoying,
little nervous ways. I think I must have,
and no doubt Alice is quite justified; and
then, do not mistake me for a moment,
Alice never says anything unkind. Indeed,
if she did I could bear it far better," —
eagerly. "I should not mind at all if she
said what she thought, for then I could
answer; but indeed you cannot think how
terrified I am at Alice's silences. Please,
Mr. Harvey, please, please do not repeat
to her what I have told you."

There was fear, almost amounting to terror, in the pretty mobile face. Amy had
risen and come near him in her eagerness.
The face between the fair waving tresses
was past its first youth, but it was pensive

and interesting beyond what it could have been in its bloom.  It was the sort of face that Harvey would have liked to paint bending over the cradle of a sleeping child; it was the sort of face to which he could not fail to pay the most chivalrous respect.

"It grieves me very much," he said fervently, "that Alice should inspire you with such dread.  I cannot think " —

"Oh, it is all my fault, I am sure," she interrupted.  "I am all nervous dreads and terrors.  I am sure that Alice does not mean to be unkind."  She went on for a minute or two trying to explain that Alice was not so much to blame as he assumed.

Harvey fervently hoped that this was so, or his own chance of happiness would not appear very great; but he did not listen with close attention to the continued protestations, for the practical question was forcing itself upon his mind, if he was not to repeat to Alice the revelation which Amy had just made to him, how, then, was his new knowledge to be made of any use?

Alice might, in trustful ignorance, be putting herself in the hands of the most unscrupulous villain. Thinking of this he remained standing by the table, Amy, in her excited speech, close beside him; and just then, as chance would have it, Alice came past the window, and, catching sight of Harvey so close, very naturally looked in.

It was Amy who started back from his side with a frightened exclamation. Harvey stood quite still, and yet it was he who suffered the more uncomfortable emotions. Amy had a weakness, which she shared with many another woman both better and worse than herself, and that was that to be in the midst of an excitement of any sort was in itself an element of pleasure.

In this particular case, however, Amy, if in search of excitement, was out of luck. Alice, who had nodded first, and then with eyes arrested stared, after a very brief survey went on to the door and came in quietly. Whether it was from wounded pride or cool indifference, she did not ask what he and

Amy had been doing in such close consultation, nor did she take the slightest notice of the former's ill-concealed agitation.

As for Harvey, he was in real distress. If Amy's tale was true, it was absolutely necessary that he should save Alice from further compromise, but with Amy's prayers sounding in his ear he could not betray her confidence. With this on his mind he sat down with the two ladies to the simple supper-table, and felt very much perplexed indeed to know what course it behoved him to take. He was obliged to take leave without coming to any decision.

## CHAPTER XIII

THAT night, somewhere about eleven
o'clock, after Harvey was ensconced in his
own rooms, he heard a tapping at the door,
and a lad whom he had seen working in the
Norcombe gardens was brought in to him.
The lad, although questioned sharply, appeared to have nothing to say until Harvey's
worthy old landlord had shuffled out of the
room; then sidling to the door and shutting
it, he precipitately laid a note on the table
before Harvey and hastily stumbled out of
the room and out of the house again. Harvey opened the note and found it to contain
a hasty scrawl in Amy's handwriting; he
supposed that Amy's nervous injunctions
had produced the peculiar secrecy of the
boy's demeanor.

The writing upon the sheet before him
was formed by such trembling fingers that,

although in the utmost haste to grasp its
contents, it was a minute before he could
do so. Without address or signature, the
note ran thus: —

"I cannot tell you how terribly alarmed
I am. Alice has gone out. She cannot be
merely in the park, for I have waited a
quarter of an hour. Perhaps I am quite
wrong to send this to you, but I am so exhausted by fear and sorrow that I hardly
know what I am doing. There is nothing
else that I can do. At one moment I think
it is taking too great a responsibility upon
myself to send this; in the next moment I
think it is a greater responsibility not to
send it, for at least I shall have done all I
can if I let you know without delay what
has occurred. Oh, forgive me if I am
doing wrong, or at least do not blame me
too severely."

Harvey had patiently deciphered to the
end with the natural idea that so many lines
would contain some further item of information concerning Alice than just that one

bare fact told at the beginning. No sooner
had he got to the end than he crumpled the
note into his pocket, and with stumbling
haste, equipped with cap and ulster and
stout stick, went out into a night of rain
and mist and chilling wind, turning toward
the combe. When he found himself strid-
ing over the heather more deliberate thought
naturally came to his mind. What reason
had he for supposing that Alice would ven-
ture through the combe at that time of
night? Then at the mere thought of such
a possibility, his heart shuddered and all
his pulses urged him to hasten onward.

He ran down the combe path at full swing
and went on into its lonely, echoing, central
parts, and there stood listening to the stream
that chattered over the rocks beneath, just
as it might have done on a summer day,
and to the drip, drip, drip of rain and mist
falling from the forest trees above him
or from the precipitous rocks below. He
shouted aloud, thinking that if any interview such as he vaguely feared were taking

place in that region his shout must frighten the evil-doer, or give Alice if she had need of help the knowledge that it was at hand. His own voice alone echoed back to him the dull unintelligible echoes met and broken by the trees. He hastened on for a mile, and came out where the stream widened under the bridge of the highroad.

It was past midnight and singularly unpleasant weather; not a creature from the village was to be seen or heard stirring abroad. Harvey's impulse was to go on through the village to Norcombe House, where at first he imagined he would instantly see or hear something to relieve or intensify his anxiety, but when he got to the gates the house stood dark and silent. Could he make a clang with the front knocker and ask if Miss Bolitho was at home at that hour? The very thought of such a course made him shrink back into the shadow of the hedge. Still more impossible was it to go round and throw pebbles up at Amy's window and make the inquiry privately of her.

It is in this that the griefs of real life, however irreparable or deadly they may be or become, differ from the same events as these appear in tragic story. In the latter, considerations which are classed as trivial, and are certainly ludicrous, are eliminated, in the former they are ever present.

Harvey tried to set his objections aside. Why could he not go up to the house? Was his errand not important enough? Was it a time to respect mere conventionality? Yet he could not endure the thought of walking to the door.

The glib faculty called self-excuse suggested promptly that such an act would betray Amy's confidence. "Bother take Amy, and her secrecy, and her cowardice!" answered Harvey. Amy's pleadings seemed to him flimsy at the moment, but only because they were brought into comparison with the momentous question of Alice's safety.

When he dashed that excuse aside a more real reason for objection came forward. If

Alice had returned, and, as was after all quite possible, with an excellent reason for her absence, such as, for instance, the illness of the gardener's wife, how would he appear in her eyes, or in the eyes of the villagers, who would surely hear of the circumstance?

His mind turned now to the dark hill, and wondered why he had not searched there. The heath had been as often the scene of Alice's secret appointments as the combe. At the thought of these secret meetings of hers, which undoubtedly had taken place, his fears revived with intensity, and he looked at the dark blank house with passionate inquiry. Either Alice had returned home, or she had not. If not, she was at that moment exposed to dangers from which he must and should rescue her. Never had he loved Alice as at this hour when fear and solicitude made his imagination vivid as to the suffering she might entail upon herself. Probably the feeling that he had had for her till now had not been truly love, and with this new birth of love was born a new power of anger for the faults that led her into risk of danger.

It is a curious thing, this power of love to intensify anger against its object, but it is undoubtedly one of the fundamental laws which govern the motives of men.

With a heart so tender towards Alice that he would without any hesitation have risked his life to help her in any way, and a mind boiling over with invective against her fault, Harvey turned from her gates, deciding that if he should go to the house and find that Alice was safe he could be of no use there; and if he found that she had not returned, what more could he do than just go back to those places where he had previously seen Alice lingering with the unknown enemy?

When he had ascended the combe he walked onward upon the moor. They had been burning heather in different places on the hills, and the smoke and peaty smell still lingered in the air in spite of mist and rain. Nothing was to be seen, nothing to be heard, but the chilly wind that feebly rose and fell, and the combe stream that leaped and rushed within earshot. Harvey tramped on through drenched gorse and heather as well as he could guide himself toward the broken cottages in the hollow. It was a very disagreeable way of spending the night, and certainly no love of excitement had any weight with Harvey. Wet as he was, and trudging wearily, nothing led him on but that fire of love by virtue of which he was so exceedingly angry with Alice, and yet hastened after what he knew to be the merest, most shadowy chance of serving her.

Having wandered, naturally enough, a little out of his bearings, Harvey came upon the cottages with unexpected suddenness and without knowing from which direction. At first they all appeared dark, and even their forms were quite indistinct in the thick blackness. Yet, looking intently, he saw smoke issuing from one chimney. This,

then, must be the hovel where the old witch
lived. Harvey stepped nearer a glimmer
of light that he now saw, and descried a
miserable half-broken window; but so faint
was the glimmer that he perceived that the
casement was covered by a thick curtain set
against it from within.

Here Harvey again hesitated. It was
strange that the witch should have such a
fire alight in her hut all night, and so carefully hidden, too, so that only one small
chink by accident betrayed it. It was very
strange! Yet he could not bring himself to
imagine that Alice could be there.

His mind reverted to the time, only a
week before, when he and Amy had thought
that Alice's first errand to this place might
have been the maidenly one of consulting
old Gor concerning her lover. The memory
gave him a thrill of sad pleasure. What
with his direful fears concerning her strange
conduct, and (if they should prove a bad
dream) his new jealousy of Knighton that
seemed by contrast a waking reality, he

dared not now hope, as he had done then,
that Alice's heart was all his own. Yet the
memory of that illusion seemed lovely to
him. He went nearer to the wall within
the shelter of the roof, and stood a moment
trying to dream that Alice was inside, alone
with the old wife, playing at cards for his
love, and that she might presently emerge,
frightened, eager, glad — oh, so glad, to
find his protecting arm unexpectedly there.
How joyfully would he pay the witch's fee!
How proudly would he take her home! It
was one of those airy joys that we can build
for ourselves all in a passing thought —
a glowing conception, a few bright details
added to make it real, a moment to feel the
glow as if it were real, and then life is
darker because of the lightning flash.

It had not occurred to him that he could
hear what passed within the cot, but he now
became aware that there was life stirring on
the other side of the wall. A hollow cough
and a moan of great weakness and suffering
was the first sound which startled him; he

almost felt the sufferer moving on the other
side of the stones against which he stood.
Then a voice began some gentle utterance.
Was it a nurse soothing her patient, or a
mother hushing her child? Evidently the
moan of pain awakened the soothing re-
sponse, and while he was wondering his
wonder increased a thousandfold, because
the words that were being uttered, terribly
familiar as they were, were finding their
way, phrase by phrase, to his understanding. The voice was not familiar; he judged
it to be the voice of an aged man, and it
was reading, without any taint of the country dialect, a portion of one of the Gospels.

"'And we indeed justly, for we receive
the due reward of our deeds, but this man
has done nothing amiss.'" Then again, in
a moment he heard, "'To-day shalt thou
be with me'"—

The moan and the suffocated cough came
again, and then another voice, thin and unnatural as with fever, "I wonder if that
thief died harder than this."

The fire that was in the wretched place shot forth a brighter flame, and through the crack in the window's covering Harvey saw, for one moment, the visage of an old man, the features terribly thin, the hair unkempt and wild. It was the face of a man as it seemed mad with suffering of some sort, and yet Harvey thought it belonged not to the voice that moaned and spoke the excited feverish words, but the voice that was reading the old story quietly. Just for one instant of time, the leap of the flame, coinciding with the movement of the head within the line of the chink, made the face and the character it revealed present to Harvey's understanding. That instant passed, the flame had died down, there was nothing but just the blank outside of the window before him, and neither tone nor movement broke the silence, although through the loose window he still thought he heard a labored breath.

Harvey drew back some paces into the heath from whence he came. Had he slept

a short unconscious sleep and dreamed? If
not, he had seen and heard a thing that was
wholly unexpected.     For a moment a sense
of its unreality came over him that almost
amounted to fear of the supernatural.

Then he settled it.   Two wayfarers, unable to go farther that night, had been per-
mitted by Gor to rest in her cottage.   This
must have been what had occurred.

Harvey felt assured that, wherever else
Alice might be, she was not there; and he
was glad to go from that place as quickly as
he might, under the strong persuasion that
if he had not been near anything more
strange and mysterious, he had at least
brushed shoulders, as it were, with the
Angel of Death.

## CHAPTER XIV

BEFORE breakfast next morning Harvey was on his way to Norcombe House. He had only, however, got as far as the village church when he was stopped by the sight of Amy, who was sitting on one of the gravestones near the road waiting for him. She began speaking at once hurriedly.

"I did not know what to do. I hope you will not think it strange that I should come and wait for you here; I felt sure you would come down before breakfast — at least, I thought it was most likely you would."

He was rude enough to interrupt: "Alice is all right, then?"

"Yes, she came in in about an hour, and it seems, although I did not know it, that she had Mary with her. She would not tell me where she had been. I could not help asking her, you know. Oh, I cannot tell

you what I suffered! When she came in I
could not possibly conceal my distress. I
am sorry now, because Alice does so heart-
ily despise women that cry; but I could
not help it, indeed I could not, Mr. Harvey.
Oh, the relief it was to see her come back."

"I am sure Alice could not despise your
affectionate solicitude, Mrs. Ross. It may
not be her way to give much expression to
her feelings, but she has a heart, and she
must value yours."

There came a set look about the mouth
and chin of Amy's mobile face; her tone
was formal. "Oh, I am sure Alice does
not mean to be unkind."

"But she was unkind! What did she
say? What did she do?"

"She went and got me some hot wine and
water. Do you know what it is to have
your heart laid down upon the floor and
trampled upon?" Amy's feelings were evidently too deeply wounded to fill up the
pause that followed with her usual asser-
tions of Alice's goodness.

Harvey was picturing the scene in his mind. He wondered whether, if he had met Alice in the combe the previous night, she would have advised him to go home and sip negus. He felt that it was imperatively necessary that Alice should change this attitude of mind, and in his joyous relief at finding her safe he could not think of this change as at all impossible. He was very much displeased with Alice; he realized that the time had come when he could no longer allow her to have her own way — no longer, that was, if she had any intention of being his wife. Her action of last night made this clear, and her way of receiving Amy's affection and solicitude could well be made a matter of remonstrance at the same time. The anger of love, if bitter, is always hopeful. He felt that a little reasonable explanation of Alice's error must work a wonderful improvement. The morning happened to be very bright. He did not look forward to the interview with dread; it was only the next action it was necessary for him to take, and a man must take things as they come.

Amy, who supposed herself to have overstepped some womanly barrier in making advances to Harvey, was already talking about her note of the previous night, and her meeting him that morning seemed to come under the same head in her mind. Although he could not see any likeness between the two actions, Amy was apologizing, and hoping that he would not think it strange, and at the same time explaining, with that hard little drawn look about her mouth, that she could not possibly help herself, for she had been driven to do just what she had done. She did not seem to have any conception that her note had kept him out in the rain half the night. As he had not come to the house she appeared to assume that he had done nothing. But her solicitude lest her communication should have caused him to lose sleep was so lively that he felt it unnecessary to explain what had really occurred. In the safety of the morning, he did not know exactly why, there was a certain light of absurdity adhering to the night's energetic vigilance.

"Well" — Harvey summed up his conclusions in this word — "I will go with you now and talk to Alice." Then, mindful of yesterday, he added, "I need not quote you, you know, if you are so averse to it."

"Oh, say what you like about me. I see I need not have troubled you about my excuses, for you are preoccupied, you are thinking only of Alice." The hardness of Amy's expression had come now also into her voice. "I do hope very much, Mr. Harvey, that she will make you a loving wife, for even I, although I have seen so little of you, have learned to value you as a friend. But pray don't think of shielding me in anything that you might wish to say to her, for I have quite decided that I cannot remain here any longer." Amy's voice faltered, but there was no suspicion of tears; her face had the dry, fixed, nervous look that tells of greater suffering. "Oh,

no, do not ask me, I cannot remain; I owe
something to my son as well as to Alice.  I
— oh, you need not trouble any more about
me.  I cannot remain — do not ask me."

Harvey felt very sorry for Amy, really
very sorry; at the same time he had perception enough to see that part of her feeling
of injury at the moment was directed against
himself, and it was this, perhaps, which
opened his eyes to the knowledge that her
threat of quick departure was an hysterical
exaggeration of what would prove to be her
calmer judgment; still, of course, this hysterical condition was owing to the way her
nerves had been worked upon the previous
night, and probably for some time past.  It
was Alice who was to blame for it.

It was some saint's day; there was a service going on in the church, and Amy went
in for the end of it.  Harvey went on to
Norcombe House to find that Alice had
already had breakfast; she was sunning herself at the front door, and Mary was down
upon her knees, scrubbing the steps.  No

offer of a meal was made, evidently because it did not occur to either woman that Harvey was fasting; he himself was intent upon graver matters than breakfast. Alice walked with him down the path that led past the brick wall of the garden, and they sat together on the old bench on which she had refused to sit on the day when they had come to the first agreement about their friendship.

The small red blossoms of the high elms had passed; a smoke of greenish gray leaflets was about all their boughs. The daffodils were few, but on the dyke the bees were sucking the golden balls of withy trees.

"Alice," — kindly, — "where did you go last night when you were out between ten and eleven?"

Alice was sitting rather listlessly; she, too, looked tired. "I should think that you might naturally argue that I would not have troubled to go out at that hour if I could tell you about it now; that if I could be open about the errand to-day, I would

have done it openly yesterday. It is you
who have dogged me day after day until I
not only had to go out at night, but very
late and in the rain. I am weary of this
system of spying that you and Amy have
organized together. I told you that I was
sorry there was need for any concealment,
and more I cannot say now. I cannot, of
course, control your suspicions, or your
efforts to circumvent my freedom, but it is
equally of course that I must judge your
character accordingly."

"And does every one's character fall in
your estimation whose actions are prompted
by anxious affection for yourself?"

"Hardly that."

"Is not that what your words imply?"

"It depends a good deal upon what actions are prompted by the feelings you describe. You would not wish it to be said,
for instance, that you could not respect a
woman whose actions were prompted by
love for you, but there are many things that
a woman might do from that motive that
would take away your respect for her."

This was very different from talking to Amy. Harvey felt that Amy had a much more womanly way of setting a man at his ease; he never felt at all at a disadvantage with her. He also remembered that he had had no breakfast, and thought that that was the reason that he did not feel inclined just then to chop logic. He was becoming irritated: he had come to find fault with Alice, and with very good reason, and instead of that she was lecturing him; there must be something wrong somewhere.

"You are quite unjust, Alice, in saying that Mrs. Ross and I are acting together to spy upon you. You speak of my suspicions — it is you who are suspicious, and with much less cause."

"If so, I beg your pardon. I cannot, of course, tell what has passed between you. I neither know nor care how far it has gone; but Amy is a very transparent person, when you know how to read her, and it has been evident by her little looks and ways for a week back that she at any rate imagines

herself in your confidence; and if you did
not meet her this morning how did you
know that I was out last night?"

"I did meet her this morning, and also
she found means of sending a note to me
when she found that you had left the house
last night."

"Oh!"

It was a little word, so quiet that it
could hardly be called an exclamation; yet
it said to Harvey that Alice was surprised,
and thought her former accusation much
more than verified.

"You are unjust," he answered, "if you
imagine that either Mrs. Ross or I have
done anything of which we are ashamed " —

"That would depend upon what your
standard is, would n't it?"

"Our standard!" — hotly. "Well, for
one thing I hold it as a principle that a girl
like you ought not to go out at night without letting her friends know where she is
going; and if Mrs. Ross thinks so, too, I,
for one, honor her for it."

Alice sat quite still; she was looking at the moss on the path before her, but with an expression upon her face as if she were listening to him intently.

"And another standard that I have, Alice, is, that a woman who loves you, and errs, if she errs at all, only out of exaggerated solicitude for your welfare, ought not to be treated, time and again, with coldness and contempt."

"Are you speaking of Amy? You assume, I suppose, that I treat her unkindly because she has *told* you so?"

The tone seemed to Harvey a corroboration of Amy's complaints.

"If she had *told* me so I would have believed her implicitly. I know enough of Mrs. Ross to know that she is incapable of falsehood, but instead of that she has constantly spoken of the kindness of your intentions, and, whenever she could do so honestly, of the kindness of your acts."

"But implied all the time that she was praising me that I was a very disagreeable person to live with?"

Harvey felt very angry on Amy's account; her pretty pleading face rose up before him; he felt more sure than ever that Alice did not understand Amy at all. "Mrs. Ross is incapable of the motives you hint at."

For more than a minute Alice said nothing; she was evidently thinking. Then: "I think we have both expressed our minds quite clearly; if we went on quarreling for an hour probably I should not know better what you think. Perhaps it would be as well to drop the argument and maintain our self-control."

"I am not quarreling with you, Alice," warmly. "You think that I am losing my temper because I speak with feeling."

"I certainly am losing mine, and that very rapidly. If the catastrophe is to be averted there is no time to lose."

"I do not see that you have any reason to lose your temper. What have we done to offend you?"

There was again a little silence. Alice's

reluctance to speak until she had had time
to weigh her words induced Harvey to mistake her self-command for inward calm.

"You have told me, for one thing, that
you consider it improper for me to go out
upon secret errands late at night. Your
telling me this of course implies that I am
either ignorant of, or willfully disregard,
all considerations of propriety. And now
you tell me you have done nothing to offend!"

"Is it my fault that you have laid your
conduct open to remonstrance?"

She went on without heeding. "You
have told me also that you have such a
standard of what womanly kindness should
be that you consider it wrong to return coldness and contempt for kindness and love,
by which you imply that my standard is
even lower than this, which could not certainly be called very high. And in this,
again, you do not see that you have given
just offense!"

Again he interrupted. "I do not say

for a moment that in abstract ideas you would not have the highest standard, Alice, but practically your conduct " —

She went on as with her former argument. "And when I tried to show you that you had no proof of the callousness of which you accuse me except Amy's complaints, and suggested that those very complaints ought to have proved to you that her ' love ' to me was not the unselfish feeling that you suppose, you assure me that I do not understand at all!" She paused here a minute, but began again.

"What is it that you think I do not understand? I will tell you something that I do understand. Neither you nor Amy have been kind or loyal to me. You knew perfectly well that I did not wish Amy to know the thing that I would have kept from *you* if I could, yet you told her. She is not able to see small things in right proportion or control her wild fancies. Ever since you told her she has suffered excitement; but that is your fault, not mine. She was

in a pitiable state last night, and I was sorry
for her; but if she had known nothing that
had happened before, when she found that
I was out it would probably have occurred
to her to discover that Mary was with me
before she went into hysterics, and before
she sent the boy out and added to her fright
by being alone in the house.   But making
allowance for all her misery, it was an entirely disloyal thing of her to condescend
to suppose that I had gone where I was not
safe, and she knew perfectly well that the
last thing I would have wished was that she
should write to you."

"You expect superhuman forbearance if
you expect your friends to see you rushing
into the worst danger, and go on quietly as
if nothing had happened."

"I have not been in danger.   It is disagreeable and undesirable to walk out at
night, but as far as these roads and the
people are concerned, Mary and I, known
as we are, are as safe as in the day."

"There I must disagree with you, Alice;

you do not in the least know what you are talking about; but whether by night or day, I am quite sure it is not safe for you to compromise yourself in the way you are doing. One thing I must ask you: are you paying that impostor from Bristol money that you supposed your father to have owed?"

"Impostor from Bristol!" she repeated; "Money that my father owed!" and then, to his annoyance, she began to laugh.

He was not calm enough to see that it was excitement that emphasized her amusement into open laughter.

"Where did you get that tale?" she asked. "If I needed to make my secret errands any longer, I would leave you the supposition as a good blind, but" — and her laughter turned to melancholy — "the need for them is over."

It maddened him that she should appear to think with regret of the stolen interviews. "I understood from Mrs. Ross that some one in Bristol " —

"I don't know how Amy may have en-

larged upon it," she interrupted, "but I
have no objection in the world to your knowing that some lunatic in Bristol has been
writing begging-letters on a plea that was
evidently absurd.  Mr. Knighton put them
in the fire, and answered the last."

"What I was going to say, Alice, was,
that if that was not the explanation of your
most extraordinary conduct it is even more
necessary that I should know what the right
explanation is."

Her tone for some reason lost all its anger
now; it was very gentle.  "You forget that
I have explained it so far as to tell you that
there was nothing in it that need distress
you."

"It is very hard, indeed, for me to believe
that, Alice."

"So it seems " — sadly.

"You mean that I should think it easy to
take your word against the evidence of plain
facts?"

"I was under the impression that you had
that degree of respect for me that " — she

hesitated, but did not blush, her cheeks were white — "that is the highest that a man can offer to a woman."

"And so I have; but there are things that no man can endure."

"What things?"

There was a short pause.

"Alice, tell me — who is that fellow that I saw you with the other day?"

"Think, Hal — is it kind of you to catechise me, when I have asked you not to do so? If I answer your questions truthfully it will not help you."

"But answer it, Alice, who is he?"

"I don't know."

"I beg your pardon, what did you say?"

"I said I do not know who he is."

He made his question more particular. "What is his name?"

"I do not know."

"Do you really not know what his name is?"

"I have not the faintest idea."

"Where did he come from?"

"I do not know in the slightest."

"You are mocking me " — angrily.

He rose in impatience, and stood before her.   Her elbow was on the arm of the rustic seat; she had covered her eyes, leaning her brow upon her hand.

"Who sent this man to you?"

"No one, as far as I know."

"Alice," he cried in pain, "you cannot expect me to believe this nonsense you are talking."

She looked up at him suddenly, her face flushed, her eyes dewy with a hint of tears. "I do expect it, Hal, and, I entreat you, do not let me expect in vain.   Try and think quietly; do not get angry; I am only asking you to believe me."   She put up her hand and laid it on his.

"I am not angry.   Why do you keep repeating that, Alice?"   And then he did try to pause and think as she had requested, but what he thought of was the impropriety of her conduct, and the absurdity of her words.   He did not steady his mind for a moment to contemplate her character as he had experienced it in all the hours of the last month, or as it was now revealed in the tenderness of her entreaty.

"How can I believe it is all right, Alice — that there is nothing for me to fret about, as you say? How is it possible that you could take so much trouble to meet a man,·when you don't know who he is or from whom he came?"

She withdrew her hand and turned away her eyes, but still she pleaded. "Will it help you to know that others can trust me? Mr. Knighton knows that I meet this man."

"Oh! you can confide in Knighton?"

"Don't speak in that tone, please. I don't know what it means. I have told Mr. Knighton" —

"Yes, I see, you object to me saying a word to Mrs. Ross, but explain everything to Knighton that you hide from me."

She did not finish what she had begun to say, that she had told Knighton only what he himself knew and no more. "Mr.

Knighton is the best friend I have now."
She spoke wearily and sadly.

"Well, I can't say I think he has been a
very good friend to me if he knew what you
were up to all this time and pretended he
did n't."

She had left the seat and was walking to
the house.

"If you begin to comprehend Mr. Knighton in your general distrust, I think we had
better stop talking," she said.   "His character does not need defending from me."

"If you do not wish to say any more, I
can only infer that you care very little for
me!"

But she went into the house.

## CHAPTER XV

HARVEY had retired within his own sitting-room, a dingy place, one in which he had never attempted to spend an afternoon before, one in which none but a disappointed man would have attempted to spend an afternoon, and it was only midday.

Harvey realized that he had been ill used. He had confided in Knighton; he had certainly had no reason for doing so but the complete respect for and trust in him which he felt. He might, of course, have perceived sooner that the taciturn manner was no sign of reciprocal trust; but he had assumed that to be merely an eccentricity, and now — Well, his eyes had been opened. Knighton had perhaps done him no real disservice; there was no harm, perhaps, that he could do; but he certainly had not helped him in any way. Knighton had not used him fairly.   Knighton was not the man he thought he was.   Then, Alice had certainly not acted kindly or honorably.   She had given him to understand that her heart was disengaged, that she would give it to him if she could; now it appeared that she had only been playing him off against Knighton, who was of course incomparably the greater catch if she could get him; and in the matter of this secret, which Knighton, it seemed, had been made privy to, Alice's conduct could hardly have been worse; she did not even attempt to justify it; she did not care for her suitor's good opinion in the least. Of what use was it to care for a woman who did not wish to be cared for? to attempt to love a girl who was indifferent to even the ordinary approval of her actions which most women desired, not from a lover only, but from every one?

When he got to this point in his surly meditation, Knighton himself appeared, to pay a friendly visit.

"I hardly expected to find you in," he

said. "It is at Norcombe House that you are at home; but as I was passing here I looked in."

Knighton spoke of the political situation. The Prime Minister had resigned; a new one had been appointed; the crisis was pathetic and dramatic, and fraught with grave issues; no Englishman could help being interested. But Harvey lacked zest in the discussion; he felt no impulse to be particularly agreeable. At last the other changed the topic.

"You have seen Miss Bolitho to-day?" This was said with a benevolent smile. Evidently he thought that there was one subject that would not fail to interest.

But Harvey had not time to answer with the cold indifference he was prepared to assume before there was a sound as of a second visitor, quick footsteps outside, quick footsteps across an outer room; and while they listened, each thinking he knew the step, the landlady flung open the door and Alice Bolitho stood on the threshold.

"Come! please come! I want help."
Then, seeing Knighton, she appealed to
him. "I am glad you are here; I want
you."

She turned, and, as quickly as she had
come, went out of the house again; by the
time the two men, making exclamations to
each other, had got themselves into the open
air, they saw her hurrying obliquely across
the heath. It was a minute before they
came up with her.

It was a gray day. The smoke of the
heather, that had been burning for some
days, dimmed all the air; here and there on
the hills near and far great plumes of smoke
rose where the burning now was, and under
it, in some cases, the red flame could be
seen. Their bit of the moor was deserted,
cold and murky.

"For heaven's sake, Alice, tell us what is
the matter!" The appeal was Harvey's.
He stood still to make it by way of forcing
her to stand still to answer.

Alice stopped a moment, turning to them,

but the difficulty of making any headway in a perplexing explanation kept her silent, lips parted, eyes clear and eager, her color high with the wind; she only looked her impatience.

"You are in haste; you can speak as we go," said Knighton.

"There are two men living in the cottage that is farthest from old Gor's." Alice spoke breathlessly, in short sentences, as she walked on. "They have been hiding there. One of them has done some crime. I think perhaps he was a Nihilist. I don't know what he did; but he was nearly caught, so they hid here. He was ill and going to die, anyway. They were only waiting till he died, and now he is dead. I am afraid the old man is going to die too, but he says he wants to speak to a magistrate"— She turned to Knighton.

Harvey was saying now that he had come upon these men last night; that he thought they were tramps, putting up for the night with the old witch. Knighton spoke at the same time.

"You have been giving charity to them for some time?"

She stopped now for a moment of her own accord. She looked down as she spoke. "He caught me in the combe one day. I thought he was mad and was going to kill me, and he made me — made me promise to keep the secret and give them food."

"Do you mean to say " — Harvey spoke in irritation — "that you have been giving charity to one of these sneaking Anarchists because of a promise he extorted from you by force?"

They were all three walking again through the growth of heather. The skirt of Alice's gown brushed its brown seeds heavily.

"And this is the secret that has made us all miserable?" Harvey, having received no answer to his former question, asked this one less boisterously, but not with less irritation.

"If it has made you miserable, now that it is explained I hope you will be happier." In a moment she spoke again to Knighton.

"The old man is not a criminal. He is dying, I think; but you will make nothing of him by looking like a policeman."

They all came suddenly down upon the hovels. Old Gor was standing, leaning upon her stick, near the door of one which was not her own. Alice went into it quickly, and the two men, stooping as they entered, followed.

At one side, on a rough table loosely constructed of boards, lay something that appeared to be a corpse, covered entirely by a woolen plaid spread like a sheet. On a sackful of straw, on the wooden floor near it, crouched an old man dressed in ulster and muffler, as it seemed for warmth. He had been sitting on the sack with his feet on the floor, and fallen over; but when they came he sat up, holding to the edge of the table with one hand. His face and hand were so thin that it looked as if the life within him was the life of a spirit making use of this attenuated frame, rather than of a living man. His eyes, bright and glassy,

singled out Knighton at once; but when he
essayed to speak he was obliged to beckon
with the other hand, that even in that small
room, they should come nearer; and they all
three drew very near.

His words were only a hoarse whisper;
he spoke to Knighton. "It concerns no one
now to know who we are. My boy, who
had the dogs upon his track, is dead. If I
live, they can put me in jail, or in the work-
house; if I die (and the old witch out there
says that I am struck with death), there is
money to bury us in the one grave, and
money to repay the young lady there for
the food she has given."

He fumbled in his breast.

"What is your name?" asked Knighton
sternly.

The old man only tendered him a small
silken purse with shaking hand.

"I want to say to you," the hoarse whis-
pering continued, "that that young lady is
innocent of all knowledge of us, but that I
compelled her in fear of death to swear by

the Holy Catholic mysteries that she would
bring us secretly such things as the son I
loved might eat and die upon with less pain
than the pain of starvation. Young ladies
should have a fair name, sir, a fair name.
I am an old man, so I saved my breath to
tell you this."

Knighton took the purse. He felt soft-
ened for a moment in spite of himself; he
did not demand the name again at once.

"Ask him if there is nothing we can do
for him — write to some one, tell some one,
something he may wish to have done *after*."
Alice spoke urgently to Knighton, and he
felt surprised that, in her womanly notions
of what was fitting at a time of death, she
should not grasp the case and see that this
man had cut himself from all links to the
world.

The sick man could not but hear her
words.

"The man that dies without a name,
young lady, makes no bequest, and leaves
message for none." He looked now at

Knighton; with Knighton it apparently
gave him some faint pleasure to talk as with
a fellow. "The investments of such an one
lie unclaimed; the newspapers say he is lost;
and the next day the world has forgotten
him. But " — he examined Knighton with
his eyes — "if you have a son live in his
world, and make merry with him; for I sat
at my books, and I made money. It was
all for the boy, and one day I found that he
had been led by devils to the gate of hell;
it is at that gate we die together. May
God save us from entering in! "

"Do I understand that your son belonged
to some revolutionary society? " Knighton
had taken out note-book and pencil.

"He lies before you," whispered the old
man sternly; "ask him what you will."

Knighton was peremptory, yet seemed to
feel the futility of his investigation.

"You yourself offered to take this lady's
life, did you not? "

"Yes; did I not tell you? " The whisper
broke now into a clearer voice, stimulated

by angry excitement. "Did I not tell you
that to the very door of hell I had come
with the boy? But, think you, when I
brought him here (because I had seen the
place once on a summer's day, and thought
that a knave might find hiding), was it the
thing I desired to draw the eye of the law
to the very place by another crime? She
repeated the oath when I only threatened to
throw her over the rock. I could not have
done it, for my own sake and his; but I
threatened — I threatened her with a direful death. The gate of hell! the gate of
hell! Do you think I did not see her after,
as she swooned with fear of me? Day and
night before my eyes I saw her! It was
all to keep the lad with me a few days
longer, and let him know before he died
that his father's heart was all his own. They
do not know that, our sons; they think us
hard."

Knighton stood still and stern. His de-
testation of the very thought of crime, his
indignation at the coercion of Alice, his

annoyance to find that these men could hide
themselves so well and so long, as it were
under his eyes — all this, appealing to the
more habitual motions of his mind, almost concealed from him what pathos there
was in the squalid scene. For they were
squalid, these two — the unseen corpse,
draped with a pall, stained and soiled, and
the old man, unwashed, uncared for, with
garments smeared, no doubt, in his clumsy
feeding of the sick.

Harvey took Alice by the arm. He was
full of compassion now, but quick to perceive the revolting details of the place.
"This is no place for you," he said gently.
"There may be infection; but in any case
it will make you ill." He tried to draw
her outside by force.

She moved with him a few steps, mechanically, but turned again, and, before they
could stop her, stooped to lift the arm that,
clinging to the rude table, was the only
support of the white, disheveled head. The
head, that had sunk upon the arm, was

raised fiercely, as if in defiance of a stranger's touch.

"I will help you to lie down, and make you comfortable," she said, with that gentle authority which is the true nurse's instinct.

But that she had tried to take his hand from the table on which his dead lay roused all the petulant supposition of nerves that were diseased with a long anguish. With a weak access of temporary strength he clung to the rough table he had erected, kneeling beside it, embracing with one arm the support that upheld it, and laying his face on the shawl that covered his son.

"The gate of hell!" he whispered hoarsely. "You and I, my son." His head sank lower.

It was Alice who stooped, trying to hold him. Knighton put his hand on her shoulder to push her away.

"We will lift him," he said.

"My son! my son! You and I together." The words were delirious. "And may God, who is a Father" — the words

ended in a long, low shriek, that told that
the fire of fever had suddenly blazed in the
veins.

Old Gor came in. It was she and Alice
who put the dying man back upon the
wretched bed; both the men were engaged
in trying to get Alice away. It appeared to
them that, if they could have got past her,
they would have done what she did; but
possibly this was not the case. In a little
while the moan of the sufferer was quiet
once more. By this time Harvey had run
with all speed back to the house in which he
lodged, which was the nearest, to fetch those
who would stay with the sick man. "Alice
must be got away," he and Knighton had
said to one another; and then there were
doctor and priest to be fetched.

Knighton still stood just outside the door
of the hovel. He regretted that he had not
made more insistent inquiry for a name that
it appeared so necessary to have. His mind
wandered far and wide over the kingdom,
through all the late annals of crime which

he chanced to have read, but he recollected nothing that threw light upon this unhappy case.

When Harvey and his sturdy landlord came, they lifted the plaid from the dead man's face for a moment, and saw that it could only be in his father's eyes that he was still a boy. He was, it is true, young, but in full manhood; he looked as if he had never had health and had been long wasted by disease.

The father lay unconscious, muttering in fever but muttering no coherent word that was to the purpose of those who for a few minutes listened anxiously. The man who had arrived from Harvey's lodgings would stay with him; Knighton was in haste to get to the village.

Harvey agreed to be the bearer of some telegrams to the stopping-place of the coach, which was the nearest office. Knighton was jotting them down upon the leaves of a note-book.

"But you will take Alice home?" said Harvey to Knighton.

Then they came up together to where Alice stooped, washing her hands in a broken bucket that Gor had placed for her. By this time Harvey had forgotten all that part of his discontent that had been mere suspicion, and all his ill humor. It was clear that Alice was innocent and had spoken the truth; it had been made clear, too, that Knighton had known no more about the affair than himself, and Knighton had left it to him to take thought for Alice. This being so, Harvey spoke tenderly: —

"I am so awfully sorry, Alice, that you had this fright, and that you have had all this trouble and bother. Of course, I see that you thought it right to keep this promise; but it would have been far better to break it, you know."

"I must be gone," said Knighton impatiently.

So they went their several ways, Knighton tramping down the hill with Alice.

## CHAPTER XVI

"MR. KNIGHTON!" This was after they had walked a good way in silence.

"I am listening."

"Does it make any difference in your opinion that he made me swear by — I do not know how to express myself — by what he called ' the mysteries ' of your faith?"

"How a difference in my opinion? I have not expressed an opinion." He felt inclined to add, "*I* do not lecture you as if you were in pinafores," but he refrained from pointing out the difference between himself and Harvey.

"Of course it goes without saying that it would have been the ' wiser ' thing to have broken the promise. I did not know until a day or two ago what sort of a crime it had been. In any case it was a terrific responsibility to take, to leave them to die there alone just because they wanted to be left alone! I could not have taken it if I had not bound myself, and to tell any one, even Hal, that they were there you know would have been equivalent to giving them up to justice."

She was speaking eagerly, her pent-up thoughts finding outlet.

"You, a magistrate, could not have let them go on hiding there. Hal Harvey could not have taken the responsibility of keeping the secret ; it would not have been right for him. I see that quite clearly. It was not right for me, unless it was right on the one plea that I had been coward enough to say that I would do it."

"I understand you are asking me if I consider an oath more binding than a simple promise. It is something like asking whether I am morally bound in a greater degree by signing my name to a legal contract than by giving my mere word to perform the same engagement. Ideally, the answer is, No, of course. The ideal man does not undertake to do anything without the fullest knowledge of all that it will entail. Practically, however, it is so easy to speak in the mood of the hour, or in ignorance of all the issues of the case, that I hold I am bound morally in a higher degree by a document, because it means that I have realized my responsibility. If I sign it without full knowledge, it is my own fault. How far this applies to the way you emphasized the promise you gave, I cannot tell."

"I don't know whether it may be called inherited superstition, or reverence for the beliefs of my friends, or honest doubt as to whether the common creed may not be after all true, but whenever I thought of how I had promised, the words he made me say did add something — perhaps the significance you describe. I felt that it would rob me of complacency to break my word until I knew these men were going to harm some one, or unless the old man would give me back my word." They were walking down the hill in haste; her sentences came disconnectedly. "He wouldn't do that; he had reasons of his own, quite clear and fixed, for keeping me to it. His reason was not one to claim my approval; but was it for me to set it aside and assume that I knew what was better for him than he did for himself? What do you think I ought to have done, Mr. Knighton?"

"Until I have a more particular knowledge of what has passed and have time to consider" —

"I think that just means, in a very kind way, that you think my conduct has been idiotic. Well, I knew I had nothing else to expect. I have done the deed, and I will take the consequences."

She did not speak defiantly, only sadly; but he thought that she was nervously exhausted on this question, and led her away from it.

"I hope that Harvey will get a horse to come back on and be at Norcombe again in a couple of hours. I would advise a novel or a game. Is Mrs. Ross well? It is a pity that the adventure did not fall to her share."

"Poor Amy! You are always laughing at her, and she really had grown pretty peaceful and sensible; but now these last weeks Hal Harvey has been playing with her nerves, administering such large doses of her favorite stimulant that when he goes she will be more wretched than it is easy for us to conceive. Indeed, it is not a thing to be laughed at, the misery of having every nerve calling out for an excitement you can't get, and " — regretfully — " she had almost lost the morbid craving for admiration."

Knighton spoke abruptly. "What do you mean by talking of Harvey going?"

"I suppose he is going. We " — she stopped a moment — " we are not going to be engaged, if you mean that."

"When, may I ask, did you come to this decision?"

"For about a week, I think, we have been seeing that it would not do."

"It is very serious; it is a very important decision. I hope you have not allowed youself to be lightly influenced."

"I have not had any choice."

"Do you mean to say that he " —

"This thing has been too great a strain upon his confidence. He actually thought I was doing something quite unladylike and unwomanly — exactly what, I don't know."

"The facts supported a suspicion that something was amiss, did they not?"

"Oh yes; if he read the facts in that way, they did. He thinks, too, that I am heartless and contemptuous."

"Has he felt that you treated him with coldness and contempt?"

"No, it is Amy he thinks I have been injuring."

"A man may say in ill temper what he does not mean."

"Forgive me for telling you all this," she said. "We all make you our father confessor. I have no mother or sister to speak to, and I am very unhappy."

"When Harvey first came here he was singularly frank and open to me." Knighton spoke in a measured, kindly way. "I did not ask his confidence, or desire it per-haps, but I was forced to feel grateful for his trust, and I should not be rewarding it now if I did not tell you that I am sure that he has a warm heart and wholesome feelings, and few men are so thoroughly honest to themselves and to others."

After a minute, "Yes, I believe that. I respect him for his true friendliness in say-ing just what he feels. I really had grown to like him very much."

He gave a hasty glance, and saw that her eyelashes and cheeks were wet with tears. He felt the less inclined to defend Harvey.

"You see," she went on, "it is not just what he said to-day. For a great many days he has been showing that what I told you he said this morning was just precisely the way he felt. It just amounts to this: when one makes manifest one's good sense and good nature to him, he believes in them; and when, by accident or temperament, one is not able to do so, he does not."

"It is human nature."

"I believe he would have trusted me if, as Amy does, I had spent my time telling him just how much I truly like and respect him, and if I had proclaimed all my good feelings and casually mentioned all I have done for Amy, explaining to what martyr-like airs she always treats me when we are alone. I cannot do it; I despise self-display. I must take the consequences."

"But we all need that treatment from each other more or less."

"Do we? But I think the less a person needs of it the more we respect him. At any rate" (her voice faltered, but she steadied it), "it is clear that, if he is able to think this of me, Hal cannot want me to marry him; and I could not respect him if he did."

They had come to the centre of the village. Knighton was obliged to leave her;

he had directions to give. He stopped at the curate's door.

He said to Alice at parting, "As to what you have done for these wretches on the hill, I would not descend to what you call ' self-display; ' but do not therefore take for granted that I think your action has been idiotic." There was a twinkle in his eye.

"I have not acted with common sense," she said.

"No more you did. Good-day."

Knighton went about his business, supposing that Alice would forgive Harvey. "It is natural for a woman to forgive where she loves," he said to himself. He did not feel that Harvey deserved to be forgiven; but that, he knew, might not be an unprejudiced judgment.

## CHAPTER XVII

During his walk across the moor Harvey
had completely regained his good spirits.
The more he thought of it, the more relieved
he felt to know what Alice's secret had
been. It showed that she was guilty of
nothing but foolishness; a little willfulness
and obstinacy too, no doubt; but all that was
very forgivable. He did not say to himself
in so many words that until now he had felt
it more or less likely that she had done something that he could not forgive; but he felt
unfeignedly thankful for relief, without asking from what he was relieved. "She is
such a dear girl," he said to himself; and
then he thought how clear and beautiful her
eyes were, and how strong and clear was the
light of intelligence and kindliness that fell
from them. His mind reverted to that period of their companionship when they had

been most completely at home with one another, after the first strangeness of it had
passed, and before the late shadow had
come between them — the walks and talks,
the drives and the fun that they had had.
He thought how clear her complexion was,
and how soothing the firm clasp of the
strong, well-formed hand that she had given
him in greeting every day. "She is a woman in a thousand," he thought to himself,
because he happened to be in love with her,
not because he could have told wherein she
was peerless. "Of course," he added to
himself, "she is severe to Amy, but every
girl has faults; her little severities will pass
away. When she is a wife and mother she
will naturally gain those tender and delicate
feelings which give such beauty and strength
to a woman like Amy Ross."

As he came back from dispatching the
telegrams, the moor cottages were on his
way, and he naturally stopped to know what
more had occurred. A knot of village folk
had gathered. They were considerably ex-

cited, because Mr. Knighton had had the place searched to see if any proofs of the young man's guilt or identity could be found, and the reason for this search had transpired. The search had been fruitless.

Harvey had need to speak to Knighton about an answer which had been returned at once to the first telegram sent to the nearest police station, and failing to find him here or at Norcombe, he pushed on to the Hall. Because he was happy he was in perfect good humor with Knighton again.

"The doctor says the old gentleman may or may not live, but will anyway probably last a few days." This was the report Harvey brought from the moor cottages, and his comment was, "He did not take delirium into his calculation. Curious if he should blurt out his own secret."

"It is a horrible and extraordinary circumstance, the whole business," said Knighton. "I did not question Miss Bolitho more particularly to-day, for I thought she was overwrought. She owned that her chief

fear when he assaulted her was that he was
a maniac.  He must have been most violent."

"It makes me shudder!  A woman ought
never to walk alone — never, under any
circumstances.    It is madness — I mean,
of course, in a lonely place.  She ought to
have told us at once; but then a girl, even
the wisest of them, does love a bit of romance and mystery."

"There is a higher interpretation than
that to be put upon her action."

"Oh, I know Alice would try to do anything that she thought noble or fine.  Of
course in this case it was an entire mistake;
but we are all very apt to make mistakes.
They say, you know, that the clothes on
that poor fellow and on the corpse are of the
finest, and on the linen places are cut out
where the name must have been.  That rug
and the tweeds they wear are the best of
cloth.  Ghastly, is n't it?  Do you suppose
that young fellow had to do with infernal
machines?  There is n't another class of

men on the face of the earth so contempt-
ible.    No doubt, if a warrant is out for
him, he can be identified."

"Do you notice that the father did not
expect to be identified himself, or his name
known?   The police must be after the son
under a false name, and may know nothing
of the connection with his father.   It is
possible, too, that they may have fled merely
in fear of detection, not knowing whether
a warrant is out or not.   If the old man
has managed his disappearance from home
cleverly, he may be very difficult to·iden-
tify.   Who knows but what they may have
friends to cover their absence, even wives or
.daughters heroic enough for the sake of
family pride to make no sign?"

"It must be a ghastly thing to know that
one might be arrested any minute, and
hanged or committed for years.   Fancy the
disgrace of it! and knowing that one's rela-
tives, if one had any, would have their pros-
pects in life destroyed!   It is rather clever
of you to throw in the idea of the women;

it heightens the color of the thing." Harvey spoke feelingly.

They were drying their clothes by the fire in a low but large square hall, off which Knighton's library and other rooms opened. Harvey looked about at the oak casements of the small Gothic windows, and at the glimpses of pastoral landscape that were seen through the glass; he found it impossible to fix his mind upon scenes of crowded town life and crimes of hot passion or distorted reason. The dead man found so suddenly in the midst of this quiet region was, it seemed, too silent a witness of the existence of horrid deeds to bring home their truth where everything else testified of peace.

Harvey let his eyes rove up and down the picturesque oak staircase. He remembered his suspicions concerning Alice, but forgave her for wanting to be mistress of this house if she could. It was not an unworthy ambition, and he felt inclined to-day to give up the idea that she had been at all dishonorable in professing to him that her heart was disengaged. She had probably got the better of her fancy for Knighton, if it ever existed. As Amy had left the matter open to all conjectures, he could conjecture to suit his mood.

"I thought," said Knighton, "Miss Bolitho was out of spirits. You intend to call there, I presume?"

It was already plain to him that Harvey had no thought of rupture with Alice. He owed it in return for the confidence that these young people had insisted upon reposing in him to warn Harvey against further blundering. "It is very hard on me," he thought, with a sigh.

"I think," he continued, "Miss Bolitho was grieved that you had not expressed your confidence in her in spite of what might be called the appearance of evil."

"Well, what was I to think? You have n't an idea what sort of things she was doing. Why, she went out last night between ten and eleven, and stayed out an hour.

Mrs. Ross was nearly distracted; and as for me, I did n't know when she went home, and I spent about half the night tramping round."

"Had she not her servant with her?"

"Well, I believe she had; but of course I did n't know that at the time. But, anyway, it was a perfectly mad thing to do. Of course, now that I understand, and see that it was only mistaken charity, and that those chaps don't seem to have been able really to do her much harm even if they had wanted to, I 'll make it clear to her that I have n't the same feeling about it. Of course" (he added this with a little hesitation) "I have been dreadfully alarmed about her. We have all suffered — suffered a great deal, and quite unjustly, it seems to me. I very much prefer a straightforward temper myself; but Alice " —

Harvey did not finish the sentence; the ending in his mind was that Alice was so dearly beloved that if she chose to keep a hundred secrets, it did not matter to him.

This was not a sentiment that would bear expression; he left his " but " unexplained.

Knighton, out of long habit of general benevolence, had had the intention of pointing out, if possible, the rock toward which Harvey was steering his ship of hope. Now his mind within him grew scornful. The man who could know Alice Bolitho and doubt her integrity was not worth saving. Some duty he had, however, to perform, and he did not neglect it.

"It is seldom among men or women that one meets with a mind so true and noble as Miss Bolitho's." The words were said haughtily.

Harvey perceived that Knighton had ceased to be agreeable. Knighton had, in fact, begun to busy himself with some letters he held. Harvey brought his informal visit to an end. An offer of tea with Miss Knighton, civilly given, did not detain him.

He did not know what call Knighton had just then to give himself airs of superiority;

perhaps there was something behind, after all! Amy Ross had warned him; now he saw that, after all, there was something in her words.    Harvey betook himself to the road.

## CHAPTER XVIII

ALICE and Amy were in their sitting-room. Alice was reading to herself; some times she read a paragraph three times and then went on to the next without knowing what was in it. She was tired and ashamed of herself and unhappy — tired physically; ashamed, because she was in the mood to see many faults and failures in her own conduct; unhappy, because she had begun to look forward with pleasure to being Harvey's wife, and now the prospect had turned out only mirage.

Amy was lounging in a large basket-chair by the fire, her mind full of the little flutterings of thought and feeling which all the information given by Alice had produced. She felt that she was taken into confidence again, and was good-natured in consequence. Alice had told her story

simply, but Amy's imagination had grasped
and dramatized its details.   For the hour
she was full of love and admiration of what
appeared to her heroism.   She felt, too, the
glow of the generosity which made her so
quick to yield praise.

"I can't think how you could have cour-
age to go at night" (Amy gave an enthusi-
astic shiver).   "I should have been frightened out of my wits."

"When disagreeable things have to be
done there is no use in thinking about one's
feelings."

"Oh, what an oracle you are, Alice!"
Amy was incapable of sarcasm; this was
praise — warm, genuine.   "Oh yes, you are
wise.   Oh yes, feeling does incapacitate
one."   This last was said with a shade of
reserve.   If Alice were the wiser, it was at
least a comfort to know that her own feelings were superior.

"I have not acted at all wisely."

"Oh, but it was so fine, because you had
promised!   And you sacrificed so much.   I

really think that Mr. Harvey was dreadfully distressed. In fact, I know he was," — here a little tone of superiority, — " although I dare say he did n't tell *you* what he felt."

Alice was apparently reading.

As the thought of Harvey grew more insistent, Amy's enthusiasm wavered a little, but rallied as her mind dwelt upon how much Alice had staked, although she thought no one but herself knew how very near Harvey had come to giving up his suit. This was Amy's view of what had passed, but she resolved to be magnanimous and not to tell Alice.

"I think it was so brave of you to keep silence when" — Amy bridled with obvious consciousness of her secret knowledge — "I don't mean, of course, that he could have been driven to — I mean, of course, just when it would have been so much easier for you to tell."

"I am glad you are pleased with me, Amy; but, if you don't mind, I would so much rather not talk about it."

"Oh, indeed I am pleased with you! Oh, indeed I would not withhold my admiration." Then, after saying this, she began to realize that she had been asked not to talk, and her good spirits drooped. Alice had not appreciated her generosity.

The longer she thought of the request for silence the more she showed herself offended.

"I beg your pardon, Amy," said Alice. "I am sorry if I seemed rude. I am very tired."

"You are so strange. I cannot understand how it is you do not like to be praised."

"But I have done nothing to deserve praise."

Here Harvey entered, and he was very soon fairly launched into the same subject. He was full of solicitude for Alice, full of gentleness; but the habit of complete equality in discussion, which it would have been impossible not to acquire in intercourse with her, caused him still to express his disapproval with all his natural frankness. His view was quite different from Amy's.

"You see, Alice, any madman or brute might demand any sort of promise from any of us with a knife at our throats. You surely would not think that, if a fellow had no means of defense to meet an attack, he ought either to throw away his life or keep the promise."

"You can read all that the ethic books say on the subject, and then you will know all that I know." Alice spoke wearily.

"I never read ethics; it is only a practical question of common sense."

Amy was considering Harvey's words and wondering if she had previously been mistaken. "It certainly can have nothing to do with ethics, Alice," she said; "it is only what is right or what is wrong we are thinking of."

He twirled his hat, and looked at Alice with a smile that deprecated his adverse judgment. "You see, in this case, over and above the wrong to yourself (which I can't overlook), these men would have been really better off in jail, where they certainly deserved to be. Living in that hovel would have killed strong men."

A fresh light had broken upon Amy. All the little withes of her basket-chair creaked gently with it. "Oh yes, Alice," she murmured; "it was bad for them to live there."

"It was nobly honorable and self-denying of you, dear," continued Harvey, in the gentlest and most affectionate manner. "I am only trying to show why I think you were mistaken, even looking at it entirely from the point of view of benefit to them."

"The cold and the damp must have been terrible," said Amy.

"There is this to be said" (Alice had the appearance of speaking somewhat against her will), "that when I first saw them, the young man was evidently in the last stage of consumption, when, I understand, air is the chief thing wanted. The cottage is not damp; they had a fire at night when the smoke was not seen; and as for the old man, he was so nearly in a state of frenzy that I think arrest would have maddened him out-

covered that his father chose shame and
death with him rather than to lose him.
The son, I suppose, if he had any sense,
when he saw the misery he had caused and
the way the old man nursed him, recognized
clearly that he deserved all sorts of evil for
his unfilial conduct alone."

"He certainly did that," interrupted Harvey, "and the old chap was very decent in
some ways, too."

"Well, I suppose that such recognition
of evil desert is what you call repentance.
I do not need to point out the analogy that
the old man saw. He felt sure that, if he
had only time to convince his son that the
love of God was like his, and greater, he
would see that he deserved to be punished
and be in a position to be forgiven. I don't
say he was justified in the means he took —
he was driven to extremity; but I do say
that, granted his belief, his standpoint is
perfectly comprehensible. *You* are not prepared, are you, to say that the poor fellow
who died this morning is not going to live

somewhere through ages upon ages, and that the last few weeks were not a crossroads, so to say, for him, and that the turning he took was not important?"

She asked this last of Hal Harvey. It was to him she had been talking. Although she spoke without any apparent emotion (just, he fancied, as she would have stated a mathematical proposition), he felt the subject to be unpleasantly solemn.

"But you don't believe all that, Alice; so why did you act upon it?" cried Amy.

"My belief does n't make a particle of difference. If I had been free to act upon my own judgment, which, because of my own cowardice, I was not, I should have had no right to coerce the old man merely on the ground that I was right and he was wrong. I could only have fallen back upon the opinion of the medical profession that a man's body is of first importance, and upon the law, which would say he must be put in jail."

"Well, of course," said Harvey, "I

merely wished to suggest that it is n't safe
to have to do with people of that sort, and
.that your very beautiful charity might not
really have been all good luck to them; but
of course it is the risk for you that I think
most of. Why, he threatened your life.
How *could* you trust yourself alone with
him?"

"And then the jail chaplain must have
known better what to say," Amy chimed in
eagerly, "and our own Mr. Jones would
have gone to see him; I am sure he would."

"Yes, in any case there would have been
no lack of ghostly counsel for the fellow,"
agreed Harvey. "But you know, Alice,
you must not think for a moment that I am
blaming you now that I understand just
what you have done. I do not blame you
in the very slightest. It is only that I think
you have not seen the case in all its bearings."

She laughed a little. "It is hardly necessary to tell me that you think that I have
overlooked the obvious considerations you

have just been pointing out, Hal; otherwise, I suppose, you would not have pointed them out. But *why should you suppose* that I had overlooked them?"

"But how could I think that you thought of all this, when you neither acted on it nor told us about it? A promise that is exacted by force is no promise."

"I think if one is cowardly enough to give a promise, it has *some* binding force, most moral philosophers admit that — how much is not defined."

For some reason she had risen up, and he, of course, rose with her, interrupting her as he rose: —

"Oh, do not speak about being cowardly." He spoke as a man speaks when there is only one person in the world to him, and his whole mind and heart are absorbed in appealing to her. "What could a woman be in such a case but terrified? and the wisest thing, to obey her terror! But" — with feeling — "do not speak of it. It maddens me almost to think of it."

"Well, I will not speak of it. I am going to ask you to excuse me now, for my head is aching. Amy will entertain you very well, I am sure."

He made no remonstrance, but went to open the door, absorbed only in the immediate thought of speaking to her on the other side of it.

"Alice!" He was standing now in the twilight of the low-roofed hall, barring her progress. "You do not think, dear, that I am blaming you now that I understand. I know that I did speak as if I blamed you to-day; but it was only because I did not know what you were at, and your safety is so inexpressibly precious to me." Look and voice said more than words.

She was glad to find some abstract thing to say — abstract, that is, in the sense of withdrawing the point in question from their two selves. "Between those who understand each other," she spoke gently, "blame is quite as acceptable as praise; at least one feels that it is usually more just and more helpful."

So conscious was he that she was neither speaking of herself or of him that he did not even attend to the substance of her remark. "When I think of the dangers and difficulties you have gone through" — he began and stopped.

His gesture showed that he wished to gather her to rest in his arms; he had put out his hands, and when she warded them off he had clasped hers.

With quiet, insistent strength she pushed his arms from her. She would have given a great deal to speak with clear dignity, but she could not; her voice was hoarse and broken, her head, in spite of herself, sank with a shame she could not analyze. "Don't you see," she burst forth, "that we are miles apart?"

Then, in some way, she went past him and up to her own room.

## CHAPTER XIX

Two or three days passed and Harvey did not get the chance of seeing Alice alone, nor was he at all satisfied with the scant pleasure she seemed to take in his advances when he came to Norcombe House. One morning, when walking thither as early as ten o'clock, he met her already upon the road. She said she was going to see Mr. Knighton. He turned, naturally enough, to walk with her.

"I think not." She hesitated in her walk and looked at him. "I think you had better not come with me. We have been about together more than enough, have we not?"

He knew now that this was the explanation of her coldness to him; his heart sank very much.

"Do you mean *that?*" he asked, like a man who reeled from a blow.

They were beyond the combe bridge, upon a bit of the road that was not busy with the traffic of villagers.

"Why?" he went on; "why? Tell me why."

"You surely must see, you must know, that we could not be happy together. Unless we found a sufficient reason against it grandpapa wished us to care for each other; but we have found abundant reason — you must see that." There was a touch almost querulous in the last words.

"You think that I was angry with you on account of those two poor wretches who are dead? You will insist upon that, and I have told you — But I am sorry I ever was so boorish as to speak my mind at all. We had got on such easy good-natured terms that I supposed you would take what I said just for what it was worth." He had been looking at her with great distress, but now he gathered a little hope and came nearer more confidently. "I was wrong. A woman ought never to hear a word of criticism, a word of blame, from her lover. You are right to resent it. But forgive me! I am a blunderer; but I see that I was entirely wrong. Forgive, and give me another chance."

There was something very winning in his self-denouncing. She smiled faintly and put up her hand to her eyes, perhaps instinctively to shut out the sight of him, good-looking as he was, and at his best just then because of the glow of love and chivalry. "What can I say to make you understand?" She gave a helpless gesture. "Oh, we can never understand one another. Let us part without further pain."

"But why cannot we understand one another? I don't know what you mean. You understand me when I ask your forgiveness, when I say that I would rather die than offend you so again?"

"But what is it you are asking me to forgive you for? What is it you will never do again? Do you think we could ever be happy on such an irrational basis as this,

that you never criticise or find fault with
anything I do?  You would be an idiot if
you thought that I was never to blame, and
if you should think it and not say it I
should despise you."

They had turned mechanically and were
walking together.

"But, Alice"—   His words fell upon
silence.  After a minute, in which she made
no effort to help him, he asked in deep mor-
tification, " How is it, then, that I have offended you, except by too great frankness? "

"You offend me now by assuming for a
moment that I could be offended by frankness, and by offering to treat me, like a wax
doll upon an altar, to artificial adulation,
rather than as any sensible woman would
want to be treated.   You have offended me
by forgiving me when you found that I
had done you no wrong, and, most of all,
by assuming that I had done what was
wicked, or, at the best, quite thoughtless,
because things happened to look that way
— or rather, believe me, you have not of-

fended me at all, because, to speak quite truly, I am not offended; but you have shown me how hopelessly far apart we are in all our estimate of what could possibly constitute love and friendship. I cannot help myself:" She turned to look at his bewildered, mortified face. "I am very sorry, but I cannot help requiring something quite different from this in the man that I am to respect enough to be happy with."

"Respect!" He repeated her word with the beginning of anger.

"Yes; in a certain sense I do respect you for what you are, and like you very much; but how could I possibly rely on a husband whose trust in me was the plaything of circumstance? When everything appeared fair, you would think fair things of me; when by chance things looked evil and I could not explain myself, your trust in me would disappear."

"But married people can never have secrets from each other. Such a monstrous thing as this would never happen again."

"And am I to go through life knowing that I hold the place of honor at your side just because it does not happen? And I fear that you are mistaken in thinking it would not happen. As long as it is in you to trust every plausible woman like poor Amy, one who has not got it in her to be plausible would have no chance with you. My faults are as great as yours, I suppose. I could not, however much it might be for my good and yours, go on forever explaining to you that I had warm feelings when Amy explained to you that I was cold-hearted; that I was truthful when Amy hinted that I was not; that I was kind even when she shows you that she is suffering from my unkindness. And poor Amy! she has no other place to call home! And the world is full of just such women, who no more know when they are blackguarding another behind her back than a trained hound knows of the misery it is inflicting upon the quarry when it takes up the scent. They all just act upon a low instinct without

reasoning, almost without any consciousness
of what they are at."

"Alice!"—in great anger—"your remarks about Amy are in exceedingly bad
taste. She only cared about your happiness
and mine. When you are so unjust, whatever you may or may not believe about it, it
is nothing but jealousy on your part."

She had been speaking excitedly, but his
tone of anger subdued hers to that quiet
which indicated despair of any further understanding.

"I am not jealous of her, Hal—I told
you that before. I believe that you love
me and do not love her at all; but I am
thankful that you and I have found out that
we cannot agree before the feeling in either
of our hearts is so great that it will be more
than a very temporary pain to separate."

"Certainly," he said, with some irony.
"I do not think that *you* will suffer much
pain, and it appears that I am indeed what
I called myself just now, a confounded blunderer, to have got so deep in "—

He stopped suddenly, as if afraid he could keep up the scornful tone no longer, and, after he had stopped, a slight sound escaped him — a sound that suggested that, had he been a boy or a woman, he would have been surprised into tears.

"I am very, very sorry." She spoke in a low voice.

He could not speak.

"If I thought I could make you happy," — her voice continued. "I could not, I know. You would misunderstand every remonstrance I could make; it would turn me into a shrew."

"Oh, thank you; you need not sacrifice yourself." His sneer was again partly genuine, the product of anger, but partly also to conceal his grief. "I have nothing but my own folly to thank; and as for you, I sincerely hope that you may be happy." He would have turned, but in his anger all his grievances against her came upon him at once. "I must say, Alice" (huskily), "it would have been more honorable to let me know from the first how lightly your mind lay to this arrangement with me. I learned to love you before I found out that you had Knighton some way or other on the tapis as well."

"Mr. Knighton!" She stopped and stood before him, her eyes wide open with the utmost astonishment, and then suddenly her cheeks went white. "You think that, do you? You think that I am so dishonorable as that?" Her lips curled with unmistakable scorn. "If it were not for his sake, I would not take the trouble to deny it, but I can tell you Mr. Knighton would never think of me in that way. You might as well be jealous of the Prime Minister."

With that she left him, and went on to Knighton Hall.

## CHAPTER XX

Two hours afterwards Harvey walked into the sitting-room of Norcombe House. Amy was there alone; he had found means of knowing that Alice had not returned.

"I have come to say good-by."

He looked so wrathful that Amy uttered a small cry. She always took in people's looks before their words, and she was afraid he was angry with her.

"I have put up my things. I shall post as far as Porlock. I am sorry if I have disturbed you, but I thought it only civil to say good-by to you, Mrs. Ross, although my going will not be a subject of regret; things will run smoother for you, as well as for every one, when I take myself off." He was in such ill humor that he included Amy in his general condemnation of those who did not appreciate him.

Her manner was most self-excusing be-cause he was angry; she could quite imagine herself guilty, although she did not know of what. "Oh, indeed! Mr. Harvey. Oh, be-lieve me! I am so sorry. Oh, please do not go and leave us; that is too hard of you."

After she had labored thus for some min-utes, he was a good deal appeased.

"You are very good, Mrs. Ross; indeed, I thank you immensely for all your sym-pathy and kindness to me." He sat down in the armchair, where it had become his habit to sit.

"Do not tell me what has happened if you would rather not," she said humbly; "of course I cannot help supposing " — She shook her head, and looked at him with eyes full of sympathy and indignation.

"Yes, of course every one must know ; there is no making a secret of it, and I am sure I don't care to."

"Oh, I am so sorry for you and for poor Alice. How she will suffer for her unkind-ness."

"Oh, I don't think you need be very sorry for Alice. She has had her own choice."

The hard little look of strained indignation came about Amy's mouth. "But don't you think that people always suffer for doing what is wrong? And I am sure it must have been wrong. Oh yes, I am sure." Her eyes melted into sympathetic tears as she looked at him.

At that moment Amy felt just as angry with Alice as Harvey did, and just as sorry for him as he was for himself. No other consideration had as yet intruded upon this hour of surprise.

"Alice misunderstands me," said Harvey; "she thinks I have been unkind, and in that she is certainly unjust. I have been a fool with my plain speaking, I always am; but no man could have been more"— He stopped, looking sadly into the fire; his whole heart exonerated him from any lack of love to Alice.

In her quick sympathy, Amy felt so strongly that she was even less wordy than usual. "Although I am Alice's friend, I cannot help seeing that it is she, she only, who has been unkind," she moaned.

Harvey pulled himself together. "Do not distress yourself, Mrs. Ross," gently. "I would not want any lady to suffer out of sympathy for me. I am well enough. I can breast my troubles as others do."

"It was wicked of Alice." Amy's chin trembled with the hard, strained, nervous look. "But, oh, there is one thing — there is at least this — that I think you will be happier with a woman who is less cold, less self-righteous — oh, what am I saying? But indeed I have thought it more than once, Mr. Harvey."

The bitter cry of his heart arose in simple reply. "But I wanted Alice."

This arrested her. "Perhaps you two will make it up," she said softly, after a moment, but less eagerly.

"Oh no, there is no chance of that. I have had my dismissal." He rose as he spoke. "I must go; the trap is waiting, and " — with an attempt to smile — "I will not distress you longer with my bad company, Mrs. Ross."

"Oh, oh, do not say that. Oh, you cannot tell how I shall miss you. There is no one else who — seems to understand me " — Excitement and a variety of feelings mastered her. She put up her hands before her face.

"It is very kind of you," he said brokenly.

"Oh, excuse me! I beg your pardon." Her forehead even above her fingers flushed scarlet. "It is only for you and Alice that I am so sorry."

But he knew that this was partly an excuse, that this was not the entire cause of her tears, and he felt the more grateful, the more moved. Again he said in a low voice, "I cannot tell you how I thank you."

Then his mind reverted entirely to Alice. He was leaving the house in which he had been so happy. He wondered if Amy's kindness to him would extend so far as to

let him know how Alice fared from time to
time. He could not help wanting to know
that. "Would you be so kind as to write
a short note to me sometimes?" he asked.

"I! Oh, Mr. Harvey, I hardly know."

She had taken her hands from her face
and turned away somewhat. To her this
appeared like a transfer of his affections,
and she was not prepared for that. She
was not proud, but she had her womanly
dignity; she was also a fond mother, and
she had her son to consider.

Harvey, quite incapable of surmising the
cause of her hesitation, pleaded his case.
"I cannot come back to Norcombe," he
said; "I shall have no means of hearing of
the place or — of any one in it. If it was
only a line, Mrs. Ross; but I would not
wish to burden you."

Still Amy hesitated with averted face.
She saw objections to complying with his
request and thought she felt reluctance, but
Harvey's injury and the longing in his voice
moved her very much. In her indecision

the notion of self-denial with which she constantly toyed came readiest to hand. She would sacrifice herself to him!

"I will." She said the words in a low firm voice; her face was pale, but it was calm with the strength of her decision.

His gratitude was so great that he held the little fluttering hand some moments in his before he breathed his downcast farewell.

## CHAPTER XXI

MEANWHILE Alice had pursued her way to the Hall.

The old gentleman who, with his son, had taken refuge upon the moor was dead. The whole neighborhood was rife with rumors about the two unknown fugitives. That morning a report had reached Alice that Knighton had heard something important concerning them. In her restlessness she was only too glad to make an errand to inquire what had come to light.

Just before she reached the house Alice met Miss Knighton, who was being wheeled about in a bath-chair. "He is in the library, my dear; just go in," said the old lady, with a bland smile.

"Are you coming back?" said Alice.

She felt an unusual longing for this placid old woman's society.

"No, my dear; not just now. I am just blinking at the sun, and feeling as happy and sleepy as a pussy cat. But Matthew is in, and you can stay to lunch."

Alice went on to where one of the library windows had been made to open down to the' gravel, a thick wooden mullion standing between its two doors. It was warm enough in these days for windows to stand wide open.

There was no truth in the rumor that Knighton knew who the dead men were or with what crime the younger was charged. More than one young criminal of similar description was being searched for by the police, but the disfiguration of death had, it seemed, removed the only positive proof of identity.

"Is it possible that we shall never know?" said Alice.

"It begins to look like it," said he.

She had taken a seat upon a low chair, with her back to the window. She thought he would not see her eyes if she sat between him and the sunshine.

"What is the matter?" he asked.

"Nothing — at least not much."

"You need not tell me what it is," — with a benevolent smile, — "but you need not tell fibs."

"I have been saying good-by to Hal Harvey."

"And you are sorry that you have sent him away?"

"Oh no, not that, but sorry that I could n't help it."

He had been sitting in his writing-chair, but now he got up and drew in the outer wooden doors of the window until they clasped together at an outward angle, perhaps to shield her from the sunshine or to shut the sound of their voices from the more public space without, or perhaps out of a mere fidgety desire to do something for her.

"Are you right to have done what breaks your own heart? Will any consideration of pride be a sufficient recompense?"

"It is not pride. Why do you say that? Is it pride to feel that I cannot marry a

man who doesn't know of my existence?
What I look like makes an impression on
him; my words and actions make some impression on him, but the thing that is I *myself*, that has some faults and not others,
that could do some things and could not do
others — *that* does not exist for him at all."
She looked up with knit brows. "How can
I make it plain, if even you will not understand?" she cried in grief. "Take the case
of Amy, for instance; her only chance of
happiness is to learn to leave off posing for
other people's benefit, and because I try to
treat her in a sensible and easy fashion, and
make life pleasant for her without any nonsense, he thinks that I am cruel. Of course
she herself thinks I am cruel too, but then
that is just part of her defect that I hope
she will get over; and in some ways I am
fond of Amy; I can take more that is disagreeable from her than from most people.
I am not surprised at Hal liking her, but
when it comes to his being convinced that I
ill treat her" — she stopped a little breathless.

"Is it not pride that keeps you from explaining to him that he is mistaken?"

"I have told him, but he does not listen. I have asked him to believe me, but he just puts my words aside whenever they do not happen to chime with his own notions. More I cannot do. I don't know why. You may say it is pride; it seems to me just impossibility, like knocking up against the limit of one's powers in any direction. I can talk to you because you trust me. When he talks to me I just feel as if the whole of me shut up, like a sea-anemone when it is poked with the end of a cane. You would not want me to marry a man who was always shutting me up like a sea-anemone poked with a stick?"

"God forbid!" he answered. He looked down at her for a moment, and then began to pace the room with a troubled face.

A tendril of a delicate creeper that was climbing on the house wall outside was peeping with small budding leaflets through the hinge crack. Alice had put her fingers through and drawn the branch to her; it was the sort of mischief a child might do, but she was not thinking of the creeper as she drew more and more of the branch off its proper place, helping the leaf-buds to unfold with her finger-tips.

"I felt it my duty," said Knighton, "to say what I have said. Your family had reasons for desiring this marriage, and it is a suitable marriage as to age and fortune."

Alice perceived the harm that she had done the creeper, and slipped down upon the low threshold of the window, trying to put the pretty green trailing thing back to its own place inch by inch.

"I have thought also," continued Knighton, "since Hal Harvey came, that *you* desired this marriage." He stopped, for he saw that the tears had begun to run over her cheeks, although she tried, with the impatient, shamefaced gesture of a boy, to brush them off unobserved.

"You love this man, Alice?"

"I" — with trembling voice — " I think I

wanted to be in love. I am dreadfully disappointed."

To hide her face she bent her head forward on the seat of the chair that she had left. He saw her struggling to bring under command the nervous working of her tears.

"Have your cry out, Alice," he said; "it will do you good."

He turned and left her there, shutting the door behind him, and took occasion to stroll upon the lawn as a sentinel, that her window might be left undisturbed.

When she was alone she grew calm. She was ashamed and angry with herself for losing her self-control, but she was too unhappy to make much of this or any other consideration. The world looked to her just then a very unhappy place. It appeared to her that all pleasure was destined to quick eclipse; that whatever joy might come to any heart was like warm days in December, that sometimes mock the spring, cheating the birds into nesting and buds into bursting, only to be cursed by the winter storm breath. And even spring at its legitimate time, she reflected, was blasted and retarded by many an untimely frost, and soon scorched again by the heat of summer, which in its turn was so quickly swept away by the cold autumn rains. And when people did fall in love they soon fell out of it again, and friendship was seldom satisfactory, and every relationship of life a fetter forged in the furnace of pain.

How could that which had befallen her be explained but by the innate perversity of fate? For the man who had come to woo her, so they would have her think, was a good man and kind, and she, a good woman, had done the best that was in her to meet him and be happy; and now there was only one thing in which she dared rejoice, and that was that they had not walked so far together on the highroad of life as to make it harder to separate.

The mind that is candid, however, cannot long see its picture of life drawn in false proportions and tolerate the mistake.

She began half mechanically to finish her task of putting back the slender branch of the creeper upon the ledge of rough stone where it had formerly begun to climb, and, while she did it, began involuntarily to wonder what it was in her that could always be relied upon to be merciful even to the still life of a flower, pitying it lest it should have put forth this tender shoot of buds in vain. She felt such real regret at having unwittingly disturbed this little bit of the life of spring from growing in its best place and way that, for a moment, in that calm of self-suspense that sometimes comes after a rush of feeling, her attention was arrested by her own tenderness for it.

Then came the hardening remembrance that Harvey and Amy did not think her merciful. She speculated for a little while upon their view of her character and actions, trying in self-despite to vindicate her discontent with the universe by assuming that they saw her more truly than she saw herself. It would not do; her heart asserted itself in pathetic self-vindication, and cried out that her judgment might easily have been at fault, but according to her judgment she had endeavored to be kind.

This thought about the young branch and her own kindness came only as an unexpected interlude in the visions of melancholy that were passing through her mind. Her thought began working upon it, taking it as evidence that life was not wholly sad, but cast aside that clue with desultory forgetfulness, and plunged by preference into the reflection that since she had been kind it was all the more hard that she should suffer so bitter a disappointment.

Knighton had looked at his watch and concluded the time was up. Twenty minutes, he thought, was as long as any healthy girl ought to weep. He came and slowly unhasped the shutter from the outside.

"Well, you will feel better now," he said, looking in upon her benevolently.

"I do not feel better; I am angry with fate. I have never had very much to please

me; my people have all died, and now, just
when I thought I was going to be happy, it
is all spoiled. I feel as if life is very hard."

"Yes, life is a difficult business. There
is no doubt about that," he said. "Providence sends many a grief to each of us."

"Ah, well, you comfort yourself in your
faith, but I, you know, don't believe in
Providence."

Certain small wrinkles of amusement began to gather about the corners of his eyes
and mouth.

"You are jeering at me in your mind,"
she said, "but I cannot see why."

"It seems to me that you have full as
much reason to believe in Providence as
Harvey and that ridiculous little widow
have to believe in *you*."

There was something about the way in
which he said "you" that made her feel
that her little efforts to reclaim Amy, and
all her little tempest of indignation at being
falsely accused, appeared comically small
in his eyes. She was accustomed to take

large views. The situation began to appear
to her in the same light.

"You need n't make fun of me. It is
not polite to kick a man when he 's down,"
she said.

"Those two misguided young people," he
continued, "not only do not trust your goodness and wisdom, but fail to see that you
exist !"

She laughed a little. "I think you are
very unkind, Mr. Knighton. The strong
way in which I have expressed my difficulty
with Hal and my disappointment in him
may seem funny to you, but you ought not
to laugh. I grant that one's own affairs
always look small when contrasted with big
ideas, but — this is very real to me."

"I am neither laughing at your trouble
nor at your description of it, which was fair
enough; I was laughing a little at your inconsistency in this whole question of *faith*.
As you say what has happened to you is
small, but it is real, and a dewdrop may
mirror the earth and sky. If you will try

not to think a word of advice from an old friend impertinent, I think you would do well to observe that there can be no demonstrable proof of character. As far as character is concerned, who chooses to doubt must. You have discovered that what confidence Harvey had in you after your innocence was proved was of no value. Does that not indicate that in all matters of faith proof would be the worst evil, putting an end to the opportunity of giving a confidence that could be valued? You have felt aggrieved at being doubted; you have found it impossible to reveal yourself to a person who would not believe in you, and yet you have made no steady effort to open your heart and understanding God-ward in order that He may reveal Himself to you. Think if in not being able to reveal your real self to one who would not steadily try to trust you, you are not suffering according to the laws that govern all spirits from the Creating Spirit down to the least spirit made in His image. You are injured; are you not inflicting the same injury, and upon a Character, if infinite, capable of infinite grief?"

She was a good deal touched at the very humble way in which he had prefaced his little sermon.

"Your advice always carries weight, Mr. Knighton, because you don't din it into people's ears. It is like air; it only rushes in when there is a space made for it."

"That is a very pretty compliment," said he; but half mechanically he was thinking of what he had said.

"In the first place," she objected, "Hal knew that there was an 'I' of some sort. I do not know that there is a Creator."

"We all know that there is a force of some sort behind the physical; the only question is, of what sort? Harvey read the indications of your character in such a way that you could not help him to read them better." A dry smile came over his face. "Mrs. Ross helped his interpretation; it is a tenet of the holy faith that there is an insinuating devil at every one's ear."

There was silence for a moment, then he said, "But enough now of the moral; let us talk of other things."

"You men are always impatient of the moral. Now I think that it is the only really interesting part of the tale."

"Do you? I always like the love scenes best, but it is the present fashion even to skip them."

It struck her as a curious confession. She recognized the fact, perhaps, for the first time that she herself had always slurred over the love scenes in books because she felt them to be objectionable, and supposed till now that every person of superior mind or feeling did the same.

Later in the day Knighton, having occasion to go to Norcombe, walked back with Alice. They talked of the latest political events, and of articles in the newspapers, and of the progress of the spring.

The spring was at its loveliest. On the high moors the fresh wind blew the smoke from the burning heather, so that it ascended in gray tossing plumes, leaving the air clear. In the meadows around them the willow hedges were clad in a mist of blossoms, silver or green or gold. The roadside elms, trousered to the ground with brush of branches, held green leaf-buds like raindrops in suspense. The blackthorn showed its crest in the hedges and in cottage-yards, the pear tree beamed with white blossom.

As they neared Norcombe Alice had anxious, restless eyes. There was a piteous feeling in her heart, amounting almost to terror of meeting Harvey. There was the hillpath by which he used to run down to the Norcombe road so often. As they approached it she glanced again and again with apprehension; but there was no one to be seen upon it except old Gor, and she, resting halfway up, waved her stick when she saw them, and hobbled down to the road to await their passing.

She had a radiant appearance. Her hobble was almost a dance as she panted to

execute the last steps that brought her down
the hill.

"Young meäster be gone post to Porlock;
I zee un go."

It was not from Gor they would have
wished to receive this information, but it
was sufficiently important to make them
pause to know if it were true.

Gor never spoke in high key, but now
some flutter of triumph made her very bold
in speech.

"Thee may call it ' witching,' Zquire,
but I knawed he'd not be stoppen when I
knawed what the old mad sdranger was
asking o' Miss, vor the morning o' the day
he cwome I catched a big black būg in my
water-būcket, an' not a feäler it had like
other būgs, an' I wer' just all in a wonder
to knaw how much blame it was to he to be
a-going, būmp, būmp, būmping 'er head
agen things when her wer' a-made that
way."

"What is she talking about?" asked
Alice; but her mind was wholly occupied

with the fact that Harvey was gone. She lingered, hoping that Mr. Knighton would ask when he went, and how.

"Shall we walk on?" suggested Knighton.

"But I tell 'ee" (the witch, indifferent to their correct indifference, estimated their interest perfectly) "when I zeed un coming an' going, I knawed young meäster might ha' been a bit sharper if 'er 'd tried, but how much sharper it passes I to zay. I did zay to I, it 's a good thing vor Zquire an' country, vor Zquire 'll have Miss; and main glad I wer'. But zhure enough, it 's all accorden to how a creätur 's made what her makes out o' things, vor eäven a beätle wi'out feälers can do better nor würse."

After they had walked away her words came after them in repetition: "Can do better nor würse."

So they went on, but not, as before, with tranquil minds. At the knowledge that Harvey was really gone Alice could have wept afresh. She could not quite understand a sorrow that seemed so unreasonable, and yet, like a child over a broken toy, she cared to do nothing just then but give way to her grief. She was also annoyed at the old woman's allusion to a closer relation with Mr. Knighton; it was the second time she had heard such allusion that day. She felt ashamed lest he might think she listened to it, but that, being as she thought, merely fanciful, bore a lesser part.

Knighton was vexed that when he had been at some pains to dispel the subject of grief it should have been re-awakened in Alice's mind. When they had passed in silence over the combe bridge and through the village, he said: —

"Of course, if you are really sure you know your own mind in this matter the trouble of it won't last long." He felt that it was rather a stupid form of consolation, only said because he wanted to be saying something.

"You think me the soul of inconsistency to feel as if the sun had gone out," she sighed; "but of course it just means that I sha' n't marry at all, and that, according to your way of looking at life, ought to make a woman serious for a day." She thought at least that this would make it clear that she could pay no heed to rude suggestions of Knighton's attachment.

He was silent, and then in a somewhat strained voice he said, "Has Harvey made such an inroad upon your peace as that?"

"Oh, no, but" — with an effort at lightness — "I only meant that I should not have another chance. I am not the sort of girl to have had this if it had not been for my grandfather; he probably had the wit to see that, dear old grandfer."

It frequently happens that when in nervous haste we try to produce one effect upon a companion's mind, the effect produced is the opposite of that intended.

Knighton opened the gate to let her pass in. "When you have had some time to compose your mind" — he began.

She wondered what made him look nervous, and suddenly perceived that she had blundered.

"There is one man at least who will do himself that honor," said Knighton; and he went away.

His words did not refer with precision to anything that she had said, but neither of them noticed that.

Alice was walking toward the house, and seeing a shady place beside the stream where one or two daffodils still bloomed, she went mechanically across the grass to gather them. She hardly knew what she did, but she was not absorbed in actual thought, for so surprising was the new conviction that had been forced on her that she could not rally her mind to think about it.

She stopped and gathered one of the daffodils. It was a fine lusty flower, not so pale in color or delicate in form as many of its neighbors, for its perianth was luxuriantly doubled; and so fresh it was to the light of heaven that the green hue of its first unfolding was only becoming golden, and its gold was as yet green-tinted. Alice held it, noting its perfection. The purling brook was at her feet; the sunbeams glinting from the green leaflets of the elms fell upon her.

Her heart was very sore about Harvey. If this new thing which Mr. Knighton had just suggested should take place (and in the depth of her heart Alice knew that if Knighton loved her she would learn to love him) Harvey would surely find in it confirmation of one at least of his false accusations, and, perhaps, think all the rest proved true in consequence.

Some dawning peace and satisfaction of heart she could not fail to feel as Knighton's affection won its way to her understanding, but her thoughts were with Harvey. He had offered her the best that he had to give, and she had thrown it back to him; so cruel it seemed that she would have given much for the relief of being able to imagine consolation for him. Even now she would have been so glad to have him back, would have

been so glad to have loved him and rejoiced
in him, if only he could have one flash of
real insight, one moment's vision of what
she saw and valued.

She looked into the future, trying to find
hope for him, yet in some way her imagination could not formulate hope.  "He will
live," she thought to herself, "indifferent to
the best that is in the world, or else broken-
hearted because he does not find the best
and thinks it is not to be found.  He will
marry some woman like Amy.  Perhaps"
(this thought slowly added itself) — "perhaps he will marry Amy."